ONE
GREAT
TRUTH

JONATHAN FALWELL

ONE GREAT TRUTH

Finding Your Answers to Life

HOWARD BOOKS
A DIVISION OF SIMON & SCHUSTER
New York   London   Toronto   Sydney

Our purpose at Howard Books is to:
• *Increase faith* in the hearts of growing Christians
• *Inspire holiness* in the lives of believers
• *Instill hope* in the hearts of struggling people everywhere
Because He's coming again!

Published by Howard Books, a division of Simon & Schuster, Inc.
1230 Avenue of the Americas, New York, NY 10020
www.howardpublishing.com

One Great Truth © 2008 Jonathan Falwell

Library of Congress Cataloging-in-Publication Data
Falwell, Jonathan.
One great truth : finding your answers to life / Jonathan Falwell.
p. cm.
1. Christian life—Baptist authors. 2. Falwell, Jonathan. I. Title.
BV4501.3. F35 2008
248.4'861—dc22
2008022787
ISBN-13: 978-1-4165-6302-0
ISBN-10:   1-4165-6302-4

1 3 5 7 9 10 8 6 4 2

HOWARD and colophon are registered trademarks of Simon & Schuster, Inc.

Manufactured in the United States of America

For information regarding special discounts for bulk purchases, please contact: Simon & Schuster Special Sales at 1-800-456-6798 or business@simonandschuster.com.

Edited by Between the Lines
Interior design by Davina Mock-Maniscalco

This book is dedicated to

. . . my wonderful mom. Thanks for the inspiration you have been to me for as long as I can remember. You were there when the homework was piling up and the procrastination was kicking in. You kept me focused, you kept me moving, you kept me happy, and most of all, you kept me close. Count on me to do the same for you!

. . . my amazing dad. Thanks for teaching me so much about life, about God's love, and about what it means to serve Him. I never wanted the day to come that arrived on May 15, 2007. I daily find myself realizing how much I still need you here, but I know you're there, and heaven's a much better place to be. I look forward to the day that I can once again hear your laugh, your encouragement, and your dreams. Until then, I'll just keep remembering the ones you've already shared with me.

. . . my four terrific children—Jonathan Jr., Jessica, Natalie, and Nicholas. There is nothing in life that gives me greater joy than simply looking into your eyes and seeing your smiles in return. Thank you for being the joys of my life. I pray for you more each day than the day before. And, I most definitely love you more each day than the day before. God truly gave me more than I ever deserved when he placed you in my home. I love you guys so much!

. . . my loving wife, Shari. To say that you are the best thing that has ever happened to me doesn't do justice to the way I really feel. You have encouraged me when I've been down, you've strengthened me when I've been weak, you've helped me when I've been behind, and you've loved me when I've been a jerk. Thank you for just being you. I told you before we ever started dating that if I ever got ahold of you, I'd never let you go. Well, I've kept my word this long . . . and you can rest assured, I'll keep my word until the day I die. I love you!

Contents

Foreword

by Chuck Colson

You will meet in these pages one of the young Christian leaders who I think has a great future and whose ministry I believe God is anointing. It's a warm and engaging story.

I often have a recurring dream: I'm running in a race as hard as I know how to run, my legs pumping as fast as I can pump them, blood surging through my veins and my heart hammering at my chest wall. I'm almost out of breath, but I see ahead of me the next runner waiting to take the baton from my hand. The dream is always the same: I end up gasping as I cross the line and pass the baton on to the next runner.

The dream is really how I see my ministry. For thirty-two years I have been on the front lines of the work in prisons, in the great battles of the culture war, and in the struggles to challenge the church to engage the culture. I've literally worked at it twelve or more hours a day, traveling the country and indeed the world as Prison Fellowship has spread to 112 countries.

I seek no reward, nor have I had a moment's complaint. I do this not to punish myself, though it's a pretty grueling schedule that I've maintained, but because I believe God has called me to it. My ministry has been pure joy, even through all the frustration that everyone encounters, because I know I'm in the center of God's will. It's like the moment in *Chariots of Fire* when Eric Liddell's sister, Jenny, urges him to stop running and concentrate on the missionary field. Eric turns to Jenny and says, "I believe God made me for a purpose, but he also made me fast. And when I run I feel his pleasure."

All the same, I'm part of a generation of leaders that is fast passing from the scene. We are looking for what in the marines we used to say were "a few good men" to lead the movement. One of those good men is a young man who I think has exceptional promise. His name is Jonathan Falwell.

Jonathan's dad was one of my close friends. I consulted Jerry on numerous occasions, including about the succession in my own ministry, Prison Fellowship. Jerry knew and heartily recommended former attorney general of Virginia Mark Earley after Mark ran for governor and, as he puts it gently, came in second. I'd had my eye on Mark Earley for a few years, so while I was disappointed that he wasn't elected governor, I was also overjoyed that he'd be a candidate for the ministry. But it was Jerry Falwell's recommendation that sealed it in my mind. Jerry sent me a tape of Mark's powerful speech at Thomas Road Baptist Church.

I mention that only because it was one of many, many instances when I consulted Jerry. I considered him an elder brother, in a sense. Though we were about the same age, he'd been at it a lot longer than

I had. We had occasional differences over the extent to which leaders engage themselves in partisan politics, but Jerry Falwell was one of the men of this generation that I most admired.

Having read this book, I now admire him all the more because I can see that he was consciously preparing Jonathan to take the baton from him when he could no longer run the race. Jerry Falwell was a great preacher, an incredible entrepreneur and visionary, and a determined and faithful servant of Christ. And on top of that, a great dad. That's a winning combination.

You will get acquainted in this book with a side of Jerry Falwell the public knew nothing of. For that reason alone it's worth reading. But you will also get an object lesson in how leaders are to prepare their successors.

Jerry did the job well, and thus his legacy lives on. Jonathan is destined, in my opinion, to be one of the great leaders of evangelicalism over the next several decades. When I have those dreams about running the race to the point of near exhaustion, I now see Jonathan Falwell's hand outstretched, ready to take the baton.

Chuck Colson
Founder, Prison Fellowship

Crisis

MAY 15, 2007, started like any other day. I awakened to a beautiful spring morning in Lynchburg, Virginia. As was my routine, I was up, showered, and ready to leave the house around 7:30 a.m. The first order of business was to deliver my four children to their school. As I drove, I thought about how nice this day would be—the weather reports called for unseasonably warm weather, a welcome change.

After delivering each of my kids to their respective classrooms, I drove to my office for a full day of meetings. As usual, my first task was to check email. One message was from my dad. He had sent it the night before, just after 11:00 p.m., which was not uncommon. I read it quickly and fired off a response. More emails poured into my inbox, and another day was off and running.

I led several short staff meetings to discuss upcoming events at Thomas Road Baptist Church, where I had served as executive pastor since 1994 under the senior pastor, my dad, Jerry Falwell. Before my next appointment, I had a few minutes to gaze out my office windows and again appreciate the lovely spring day. The sun was shining brightly and there was not a cloud in the sky. I basked in that sunshine, unaware that just a few minutes after the next appointment, my life would change forever.

It began when my mother phoned to say that Dad was "missing."

Missing? I actually laughed under my breath. How could my dad be missing? As pastor of one of America's largest churches and chancellor of one of the world's largest evangelical universities, he typically had a group of people with him. Even when driving around campus "alone," everyone noticed him. How could he be missing?

I asked Mom to elaborate. She told me that Dad hadn't arrived at a scheduled meeting twenty minutes earlier, and she had been trying unsuccessfully to reach him on his cell phone. I wasn't overly concerned. Dad frequently did media appearances that required him to turn off his cell phone, and sometimes he simply forgot to turn it on again. I assured Mom that this was likely the case but that I would find him somewhere on campus and have him give her a call. If only that had been the way things turned out.

Less than a mile away, a drama was unfolding in my father's office. Moments before she called me, Mom had called Dad's long-time secretary, Kathy Rusk, to see if she knew where he was. Kathy hadn't heard from him either and thought it strange for him to be missing the meeting, as it was a regular weekly event. She asked a couple of guys who worked with my dad in the historic Carter Glass Mansion to go into his office to see if he was there. When they walked into the room, they found my dad lying on the floor. He wasn't breathing.

A Liberty University police officer who was in the building immediately began CPR. Emergency personnel were then called and quickly arrived on the scene; they continued CPR. At about that time, I called Kathy to begin tracking down my dad. Amanda Stanley, who worked with Kathy in my dad's office, answered the phone. With noticeable reservation, she said, "Jonathan, you probably need to come over here." I immediately sensed that something was wrong. Without asking what was happening, I dropped the phone and ran out of my office. I called out to a coworker that I needed his car right away, as a friend had taken mine to the shop. Together we ran out of the office and jumped into his car for the one-minute ride to Dad's office.

As we drove across the campus, my mind raced with images of what I might find. A couple of years earlier, Dad had experienced some episodes with his heart that resulted in his being placed on a ventilator for several days each time. I thought this might be a similar situation—that he would be in the hospital for a few days and that we may need to get him to a specialist to find out what was really going on. My mind also went back just a few days to the previous Friday, when Dad, Mom, and I sat in the office of Ron Godwin, Liberty University's vice president, discussing his condition. Dad told us that he felt himself getting weaker: he had a hard time walking short distances without getting winded. I suggested that he go to the Cleveland Clinic right away for evaluation, but he decided to wait until after Liberty University's graduation the following weekend. "I can't let the students down," he said.

I didn't know what I would find at Dad's office, but I certainly wasn't prepared for the reality. As we were still coming to a stop, I leaped from the car and ran inside the office complex. I arrived at Dad's office to find him on the floor with several rescue personnel working feverishly over him. For a moment I stood in utter shock. I couldn't believe what I was seeing. I wasn't expecting him to be needing CPR.

Staring dazedly around the office, I saw the worried faces of the men who had discovered Dad. The conference table that always sat in the middle of the room had been swiftly pushed aside, the chairs turned over as the rescue workers rushed to begin resuscitation efforts. The room looked as though a fight had broken out. Unfortunately, the only fight going on in that room was a fight for life.

I went to Dad's side, grabbed his hand, and began pleading with him to open his eyes. I'd never felt more desperate and alone in my entire life. On my knees, I called out to God, begging him to spare my dad's life. I continued urging Dad to respond, telling him that we needed him. I told him that we weren't willing to let him go yet. I kept talking to him, the same words pouring out of my mouth over and over. "Come on, Dad, wake up. We need you!"

Still nothing.

Just then my cell phone rang. I tossed it across the room to someone who answered it and told me it was my wife, Shari. I reached for the phone and attempted to speak, but my words stuck in my throat. Tears were now falling, and I could barely talk. Shari laughed, thinking that I was playing some sort of joke on her. I tried again to speak, but the only words I could get out were, "Dad's not breathing; go to the hospital." She stopped speaking. A brief pause, and then, "Are you serious?" She said she would meet me there.

I hung up and turned my attention back to Dad. Looking into his face, I saw that he was not responding. I watched his chest for some sign of breathing as the CPR continued. But his only movement was by force under the hands trying to revive him. I decided to check his wrist for a pulse, but before I did, I prayed that one would be there. It wasn't. Tears began to stream down my face as reality set in. My dad—my friend, my mentor, my valued adviser, my hero—was dying.

More staff members rushed into the office, among them Dr. Ron Godwin, the man with whom Dad had worked for thirty years. Ron had met Dad for breakfast that morning at the local Bob Evans restaurant. He told me that he had been with Dad just a little more than an hour before, and he'd seemed fine. He came over to where I was kneeling and placed his hand on my shoulder. Though the CPR continued, we both knew it was over. I looked up at him as he bowed his head in disbelief.

More Lynchburg emergency medical services staff arrived and began performing other procedures on Dad in hopes of gaining a response. IVs were inserted into his arm. Monitors were employed to measure any change in his condition. For a brief second, they stopped CPR to see if there was any response on the screens. Still nothing.

I asked someone in the room to call Jerry Jr., my brother, and have him pick up our mom and meet us at the hospital. I sent for my sister, Jeannie, who was two hours away in Richmond, where she works as a surgeon. I asked one of our staff members to drive to Liberty Christian Academy, where my brother's and my children were, and take them to the hospital as well. I knew this would be a day like no other we had ever faced and realized that we needed to gather the family together quickly. We would all desperately need one another very soon.

Still more rescue personnel entered the room, now with a stretcher. As they moved Dad onto it, I again looked for signs of life, but in vain. I continued to hold Dad's hand. I continued to pray to God. I looked to Ron for encouragement, but he was lost in his own grief and shock. The medical personnel quickly moved the stretcher to the outside door of Dad's office. An ambulance was waiting just steps away on the lawn.

Outside, a crowd had already gathered. A local television station even had a camera crew there. I yelled out to one of the police officers to move the crowd; I didn't want them to see Dad this way. I didn't want them to know what was happening. In the dreamlike atmosphere, I felt that if others didn't know what was happening, everything would be all right.

I climbed into the front seat of the ambulance that would transport Dad to the hospital, and we began moving slowly through the campus streets. Eerily, a number of people lined the sidewalks, their faces drawn in disbelief as they watched the ambulance go by. *No!* I thought. *This can't be happening.*

As we sped along the streets of Lynchburg with sirens blaring, I watched, through the small window that separated us, the continuing efforts to bring Dad back to life. I asked the paramedics if anything had changed. One of the men shook his head. I continued to pray.

We arrived at the hospital just as Shari and her parents were walking up to the emergency-room entrance. She met me as I emerged from the vehicle, and we watched as they brought Dad into the ER. I walked alongside the stretcher, continuing to hold his hand, continuing to pray. There was no movement, no response on the monitors, and no positive words from the emergency medical services crew.

Inside the ER, twenty or thirty people stood in absolute silence. They were all looking at the man on the stretcher, the man they were used to seeing walk the halls of this same hospital to visit others who were sick, the man they saw regularly on television or in the pulpit. Now this larger-than-life personality lay lifeless on a stretcher.

Dad was rolled into an ER bay, and numerous medical personnel sprang into action. They attempted various procedures to revive him, but nothing was working. I knelt on the floor next to Dad, holding his hand, begging him to wake up. I watched the monitor on the wall . . . it never changed from a flat line. I looked around the room and noticed the grim faces of those around me. I looked down at Dad's hand and began to pray again.

One of the doctors then leaned over to me. "Mr. Falwell."

I stopped him before he could go on, sensing what he was about to say. "Can you please wait for my mom to get here?"

He nodded, and we waited.

Several minutes later, Jerry Jr. and Mom arrived. Mom came to the side of the bed where I was kneeling, tears streaming down her face. A nurse brought a chair so she could sit next to Dad. Mom tenderly held his hand, and we waited.

None of us knew what to say. None of us wanted to speak. All of us stared at Dad in our heartache.

At about that time, Dad's doctor, who had been elsewhere in the hospital, rushed into the room and said that he would like to try another procedure, but they would have to move Dad to the cardiac lab down the hall. Mom gave her consent, and we watched as they rolled Dad out of the room. In my heart, I had already resigned myself to the fact that Dad was not coming back to us.

A while later Jeannie arrived from Richmond, and we greeted her with hugs and tears. Soon the doctor returned and began to explain what I already knew. He had tried everything possible, but nothing had worked. Dad was gone. And though I really had known that when I knelt next to him on his office floor, at the finality of this announcement a rush of tears poured out of me.

———————————

IT'S BEEN over a year since Dad died, and I will admit that the tears still haven't completely stopped. He was such a wonderful father, and so many things about him come to mind each day. I miss him more than I could ever adequately express.

Dad used to say, "The Christian life means living from one tragedy to the next." His death was a great tragedy for our family. And not long after he was gone, I found myself literally wondering what to do next. I felt as if a gaping hole had been ripped open in my heart. The pain was extraordinary; it gripped me like nothing I'd ever experienced. Strangely, the only thing that distracted me from the pain was fear of what would happen now that Dad was gone. I didn't know what I was going to do or how I was going to do it. And I literally wondered if I would be able to continue.

This is truly how I felt, and even I couldn't believe it. I had always felt in complete control of my emotions and that nothing could ruffle me or slow me down. How could I have been so wrong about myself? I began to think I was not up to the task for which Dad had trained me or to the calling God had placed on my life. And I began to realize some tough truths about myself.

I am weak.

I'm not nearly as strong as I had always assumed. Realizing this was in no way comforting. In fact, it increased the level of fear I'd already been feeling. And it would only get worse—soon—because in just a few days I would be standing in the Thomas Road Baptist Church pulpit for the first time after Dad had gone to be with the Lord.

My mind was racing. What would I say? What scripture would I cite? How could I possibly find something to share that would encourage the hurting people there? More fundamentally, how could I find encouragement for my own heart and soul? I had no good answers.

—————

MAY 19, just four days after Dad's death . . . in less than twenty-four hours I would be required to stand up before more than ten thousand people, and potentially millions more through television, and comfort them. While my heart was breaking, I knew I needed to offer something inspirational to these people who loved Jerry Falwell. And I hadn't a clue how to do that.

I was drowning in grief. Dad has always been my hero, and I needed him now. But he was gone. How could I encourage others when I didn't even feel like talking to anyone? I didn't feel like helping anyone. *I'm the one who needs help,* I thought. *I'm the one who needs to be encouraged.* Yet this responsibility was upon me, and only hours remained until I had to meet it.

This was a day I had always dreaded, a day I'd almost convinced myself wouldn't really come. Although I knew that Dad wouldn't live forever, I wanted to believe he would. In recent years I'd seen him slow down a bit. He didn't walk as fast as he used to. He didn't have the mind-boggling energy for which he had always been known and admired. Although he still could preach with amazing power, he had slowed noticeably. Still, a part of me felt and hoped that he might live forever. I imagine many children who are close with their parents have felt the same. But life just doesn't work that way.

To me, Dad was superman. I always felt safe when I was around him. He was always in control. When he walked into a room, you could feel his presence, like a giant, friendly bear. He kept a grueling schedule, flying from city to city and speaking dozens of times each week. Never did that pace seem to bother him. It was a running joke among staff members that those who were years younger couldn't hope to keep up with him. But as the old song says, "The strongest oak must fall."

Funeral arrangements were in place. Schedules were set. Dad was lying in repose in the Arthur S. DeMoss Learning Center on the campus of Liberty University, and thousands of people had already visited in order to pay their respects to this amazing man. Television trucks and scores of reporters had converged on our church parking lot. Amid the hubbub, I still had no idea what I would say. The fear began to overwhelm me.

I sat at my dining-room table with Charles Billingsley, our church's worship leader and a dear friend, discussing the two services for the next day. We attempted to plan the service, but we were getting nowhere. We talked about what my sermon might be. I even pulled out a sermon Kathy Rusk had found in Dad's desk that he delivered fifteen years earlier, by his own account the message he would want to leave the world. Yet after reading it, we knew this wasn't the sermon that was needed the next day.

Shari joined us, and we continued talking about what words might comfort the thousands who would attend the funeral. Yet I still felt consumed by my own need—who could say the words I needed to hear to comfort my aching heart?

Earlier in the week, Mark DeMoss, a longtime family friend and former assistant to Dad, had come to town to be with our family. He told me about what Dad said at the funeral of Arthur S. DeMoss, Mark's father's and one of my father's closest friends. Mark recounted how Dad stepped to the microphone and quoted Joshua 1:1–2. "After the death of Moses the LORD's servant, the LORD spoke to Joshua son of Nun, Moses' assistant. He said, 'Moses my servant is dead. Therefore, the time has come for you to lead these people, the Israelites, across the Jordan River into the land I am giving them.' "

I was struck by those verses because they suggested that even after the death of Moses, that dynamic leader who had led millions out of captivity in Egypt, God still had a vital plan for his followers. Could that be true for us as well? Could it be that even after the death of Jerry Falwell, God still had great things in store for those of us left behind to continue the ministry he began?

To me, it seemed those verses were what the church needed to hear. They undoubtedly were what I needed to hear. I began to see that if God had a plan for Israel following Moses' death, surely he had a plan for Thomas Road Baptist Church following the death of its founder. And he certainly had a plan for me. I started to allow God to envelope my heart, and I was comforted to know that he would not forsake me, especially at this time when I needed him most. And God began to reveal himself to me in ways I never dreamed possible.

As if a spark had been set off inside me, I announced to Charles and Shari that my first sermon following Dad's death would be from Joshua 1. God had given me a course of action. Charles and I discussed the music and order of service, and then he left. Shari and the children all went off to bed. I sat alone at the table. I needed to take those wonderful verses and apply them to my life in order to find inspiration for my soul. Only then would I be able to honor my father, honor God, and hearten the Thomas Road Baptist Church family.

A little while later I picked up the phone to call Ergun Caner, president of Liberty Baptist Theological Seminary, and asked him to look over the sermon I had written. I explained that I was physically and emotionally spent and was second-guessing my ability to think clearly. I emailed my notes to Ergun and waited for his response.

When his response came, his words changed my life. Here is what he wrote:

> Jonathan, look at these words by Charles Spurgeon Jr.,
> the son of Spurgeon, spoken to his church at South Street
> Baptist Church in Greenwich, England. They echo the
> same heart you have shown in your sermon. . . .
>
> "What my Father has been to me, to many thousands,
> and the world at large, none can ever fully estimate. There
> was one trait in his noble and godly character which,
> among many others, always shone out. . . . His humility.
> Words of eulogy concerning himself were painful to him;
> his creed in this, as in all other matters, being 'Not I, but
> Christ.' "

There, in the midst of that quote from more than one hundred years ago, were the words I knew would guide me for the rest of my days. Those words, drawn from Galatians 2:20 (KJV), would help me to stand in the pulpit in a few hours and claim an everlasting promise. Four simple words had taken root in my soul: "Not I, but Christ!"

My heart began to stir with anticipation, replacing the fear that had stricken me for several days. Not only had my spirits been buoyed, but I knew God had planted within me the message I could share with our anguished congregation that so loved my father. I realized that God had a plan and was working it through me. What a humbling experience! God, who does not make mistakes, was active within me, molding me to accomplish his plan. I knew that as long as I focused on him and not on my feeble abilities, everything would be fine.

Just as I had felt safe as a little boy with my father, I now felt the loving arms of my heavenly Father embrace me. God was alive in my heart, and I had nothing to fear.

"Not I, but Christ" has become the hymn of my heart. I believe in, stand upon, cling to, and talk about this verse many times every day. It has become my passion. And since that night, when those words became real in my heart, nothing has been the same!

LifeTouch

LIFE IS not easy. We wake up in the morning not knowing what the day may bring. One day it may be that one of the kids gets sick. Another day may bring pressure from the boss at work. Still yet another may bring bad news from the doctor. When my dad passed away on a bright and sunny day in May, it was a day like any other day, but the events of the day changed my life forever.

From the tragedy came lessons that I could not have learned in any other way. The first lesson that I learned was that God is in control. Nothing happens without his permission. The second lesson that I discovered is that God has a plan for my life. It is a personal plan that is intended just for me. The third thing that I realized was that God will not put more "on" me than he will put "in" me to go through the challenge. He is a heavenly Father who loves us and will not leave us alone when we go through trials and tribulations.

I don't know what you are struggling with right now, but this I know, if you turn to God for help during the crisis . . . he will be there for you and He will be there with you.

QUESTIONS TO CONSIDER

1. How does the idea of God being "in control" help us when we face trials?
2. When you go through challenges, who do you turn to for strength and encouragement?
3. What lessons have you learned when you've gone through some dark days in your life?

UPWARD LOOK:

Dear God, thank you for sending trials my way. I know that you love me and that you have a plan and a purpose for my life. I also know that you have a purpose for the trials that I have gone through and the trials that I will face in the future. Give me not only the grace I need to go through the challenge, but also the grace to realize the lessons that you want me to learn. In Jesus' name, amen.

2

Not I, but Christ

THE WORDS FROM Ergun Caner's email continued to rattle around in my brain. I read them over and over again, each time focusing on those four words: "Not I, but Christ!" I couldn't get them out of my mind. I reached for my Bible to read the passage where those words appear. "I am crucified with Christ: nevertheless I live; yet not I, but Christ liveth in me: and the life which I now live in the flesh I live by the faith of the Son of God, who loved me, and gave himself for me" (Galatians 2:20 KJV).

What a verse! In the midst of the storms of life, we have someone on whom we can depend no matter what trials we face. We have someone who will restore us when it seems our hearts have been ripped apart. We have someone who will love and strengthen us when we are gripped by fear and loneliness. In those moments when

17

we feel as if we don't have the power or courage to continue, Christ becomes our strength and our deliverer. The Christ of the Bible, the creator of the universe, wants to be uniquely active in our lives. That is an amazing truth! He actually wants to help us in our time of need. He wants to comfort us when we are racked with pain. He wants to encourage us when we're desperate for help. In him we find everything we could ever need to make it through life.

As I continued thinking about the sermon I would deliver in just a few hours, only days after my dad's death, I felt more at ease. Just hours earlier I had sat dumbfounded as to what to say in that pulpit. Now I was actually looking forward to speaking because I had found something real to say that could actually help thousands of hurting hearts . . . not the least of which was my own.

This sermon would need to lift the spirits of those who would gather at Thomas Road Baptist Church. It would need to encourage those who were grieving Dad's loss. I knew this message needed to give hope to many who were desperate for a touch from the Almighty. And at last I was starting to believe that the words on the computer screen in front of me would do just that, and more. Most of all, I knew it would be a message that would give me hope in what had been the darkest hours of my life.

A heavy mantle had fallen upon my shoulders. Dad founded Thomas Road Baptist Church in 1956 with thirty-five adults. The church had grown to more than twenty thousand members, and many different ministries had sprung forth from it. Liberty University, which Dad founded in 1971 out of Thomas Road Baptist Church, had now grown to more than ten thousand resident students, with another twenty-three thousand students in our distance-learning programs at the time of his passing. Many other ministries, such as the Elim Home for alcohol- and drug-addicted men, the Liberty Godparent Home for unwed mothers, Liberty Christian Academy, and others had emanated from within the walls of Thomas Road Baptist Church through Dad's nearly fifty-one years of heaven-inspired vision.

But the visionary was gone. People would now be looking for leadership into the future. While I was fully aware that I could never be just like Dad, I also knew that I didn't need to be. Those simple words from the book of Galatians had given me the freedom to be me. I could lean on those words as I focused on the abilities and vision that God would give to me. God gave Jerry Falwell a vision for ministry, and I knew he would do the same for me. It probably would not be the same vision, but in God's economy, it would be just as important to his kingdom.

All of us have callings that God has placed upon us, and when we accept that our own callings will be different from the ones he places on others, we find freedom. There is unique freedom in the words "Not I, but Christ." Those words afforded me the freedom I desperately needed following Dad's death. They provided the freedom Jerry Jr. needed as he stepped into the role of chancellor at Liberty University, the role held by our father since the school's founding in 1971. They provided the freedom Mom needed as she faced life without her husband of forty-nine years. And they provided the freedom Jeannie needed, as her father would no longer be there to offer his advice and counsel and unconditional love.

Other Bible passages also began to come alive in my life as never before. I've already mentioned how encouraged I was at the words of Joshua: "I promise you what I promised Moses: 'Wherever you set foot, you will be on land I have given you' " (Joshua 1:3). I had heard Dad quote that passage many times through the years. He often shared the story from the pulpit how, when he was first starting Liberty University, he would walk around the mountain upon which Liberty's campus now sits. He would walk that mountain, all the while claiming that very scripture. If God could give land to the Israelites, Dad believed that God would give this land to our church to start a university that would train young champions for Christ. I love to picture Dad striding across the mountain, talking to God and knowing in his heart that a mighty Christian university would one day stand in that place. Dad never doubted God's promises. He simply believed them, claimed them, and experienced them in a real way.

While I'd heard that story many times, it began to take on new meaning. I knew that God's promises would have to be claimed by all of us who were left to carry on Dad's work. I knew that we must read those verses anew and take God at his Word that he would give our church a brand-new land—not physical land but spiritual land. Ours would be a spiritual conquest. We would be depending on God to lead us into the future.

As I continued to ponder the wonderful words found in the book of Joshua, I stumbled across even more promises that we could depend on in that difficult time. They seemed to leap off the pages, as if God were literally speaking just to me. Joshua 1:5–7 says,

> No one will be able to stand against you as long as you live. For I will be with you as I was with Moses. I will not fail you or abandon you.
>
> Be strong and courageous, for you are the one who will lead these people to possess all the land I swore to their ancestors I would give them. Be strong and very courageous. Be careful to obey all the instructions Moses gave you. Do not deviate from them, turning either to the right or to the left. Then you will be successful in everything you do.

God will be with us! He will protect us against any enemy we might face. Can we ask for a better promise than that? I knew I would be leaning on those words in the days to come and that they would allow me to get past the pain that had been thrust on my heart just a few days earlier. I would be counting on these promises, and I knew that our church needed to do the same. If I could get up each morning with the knowledge that God is with me, that he will guide my steps and direct my paths, I cannot fail. Why? Because it means that someone far greater and far more powerful than I is at the wheel of my life.

Isn't that what we all need in our lives? The concept "Not I, but Christ" can give every single person a radically transforming experience in his or her everyday life. Even when we're not facing life-altering situations, such as losing a loved one, God still wants to be present in our lives, guiding our steps, soothing our pains, and blessing us. Why would anyone want to go through life on his or her own? God, right there in the pages of the Bible, is crying out to all of us, "Let me help you!"

We don't stand alone when we traverse the steps of life. We don't stand alone when we talk about Jesus Christ to someone we meet. We don't stand alone, even when we feel completely abandoned. We don't stand alone when our families are in trouble or our marriages are falling apart. God wants to help us through every challenge in life. He wants us to lay our burdens at his feet. Joshua chapter 1 allowed me to understand that Christ would help me to carry the new burden that had been placed on my shoulders. And I knew that with his help, everything would be just fine.

THE NEXT morning the alarm jolted me from a deep sleep at six o'clock. I quickly showered, all the time thinking about those words:

"Not I, but Christ." I knew I had to center my thoughts on that truth.

I drove to church alone that morning. The silence in the car made it too easy to dwell on having to stand before our church body and speak. To get my mind off of that daunting task, I tuned the radio to a local Christian station. That morning, at the precise moment I turned the radio on, a song was playing that I needed to hear. The lyrics are, "Better is one day in your courts, better is one day in your house, better is one day in your courts than thousands elsewhere."

I imagined Dad walking through God's house that day, and I was captivated by what he must be seeing. I thought about him walking through those gates of pearl and stepping upon streets of gold that the Bible so vividly describes. How wonderful that must be. My dad spent fifty-five years serving God. He spent decades telling others about heaven. And now he was there. He was experiencing what he had so passionately taught about throughout his ministry. Once again, God had provided me with words to comfort my soul.

The song ended, and I was jolted back to reality. My stomach churned as I approached the church parking lot and the prospect of standing in the pulpit became increasingly real. Sure, I knew what I was going to say. But I still would have to step behind the pulpit where Dad had stood only days earlier. This would be the first time, and I knew it would be tough. But I focused again on the four words that had been emblazoned upon my heart: "Not I, but Christ."

As I climbed the stairway to my office on the second floor, each step seemed to be three feet tall. I settled in for some time of prayer and a final review of the sermon. I wanted to make sure that what I was feeling, the promises I had read, had been properly conveyed on paper.

A short while later, as I walked through the church complex, I noticed that everything seemed strangely different. The halls were empty; it was almost surreal. I could feel the starkness starting to overwhelm me. I had thought I was ready to preach, but the weight of what was ahead again pressed down on me. In about an hour and a half I would have to stand in that pulpit and deliver God's message to the people. My pulse quickened with that thought. I had to settle down. I had to take the words I'd been pondering and put them into practice: "Not I, but Christ!"

I prayed that God would keep those words in my heart and prevent my own mind from betraying me. Then I made my way to the worship center, where a throng of people had gathered. Even so, the backstage area was eerily quiet. Though hundreds of people from our praise team, choir, and orchestra milled around, no one seemed to be talking. It was virtually silent. I could feel every eye in the room fixed on me. I knew what they were thinking: *Can he do it? Will he be able to speak today? Will he be able to lead us into the future?*

I had already asked myself the same questions. Their apparent thoughts were the same ones that had been racing through my mind for the past five days. Would I be able to do this? I didn't have a clear answer at this point. I could feel my emotions welling up as I crossed the room. Many people offered condolences as I moved toward the backstage office. Others simply patted me on the back, not really knowing what to say. Tears were visible on many faces. This was a tough day for everyone, to be sure.

The other pastors and I gathered in the backstage office. I looked into their faces and confessed that I desperately needed their prayers. We formed a circle and began asking God for his special power in all of our lives. We begged God to make his presence known that day more than ever before.

As each pastor offered prayers for our church, for my family, and for me, I simply listened—and became more emotional with each word. As we took turns around the circle, I knew it would soon be my turn. In a way, I was relieved that I would have to pray in this small group, even though my emotions were getting the best of me. If I could speak here, with my friends and coworkers, perhaps it would be easier to then do so in front of the thousands who had gathered in the worship center.

And so, everyone had prayed except for me. I paused. I don't know if the others could feel how tense I was. My mind raced, searching for the words I wanted to say. The flip side of my hopeful theory became apparent: if I couldn't even utter a prayer in that little room with a few fellow pastors, how would I be able to preach to the masses?

I uttered a simple supplication: "Lord, I can't do it, but you can. So please, do it. Amen." That was it. Not much of a prayer. But those words expressed exactly what I needed at that moment: supernatural strength to make it through the day.

The Bible tells us that "with God everything is possible" (Matthew 19:26). My prayer had been brief, but it came from my heart. I was like a child needing his father to help him through an overwhelming situation. And our heavenly Father blessed that simple prayer. He gave me the strength to do what I needed to do next: encourage thousands of souls who urgently needed a touch from God. It was solely through the power of God that I was able to preach that morning—and since that day.

"Not I, but Christ."

I'm not going to tell you that it was an easy sermon to preach. It wasn't. But I know that God reached down that morning and, through his wonderful grace, touched my heart, enabling me— through my obedience and full dependence on him—to preach a message that honored my father and, most importantly, honored Christ. At the conclusion of that service and the identical service that followed at 11:00 a.m., God showed up in amazing ways. Thousands of people gathered at the front of the auditorium for a special prayer time for our church. We all knew that our future depended on God's power, and we were asking for just that.

And so, there it was, the one great truth that changes everything. The one truth that can be counted on no matter what the situation. Sure, I'd heard those words before. I'd read the scriptures that tell us who God is and what he can do in our lives. But I had never so desperately needed to depend completely on that truth until that day. Somehow those words became more real . . . more vibrant . . . more enriching on that day.

It seems we can never truly understand how much we need God's power in our lives until, in the midst of intense pain or loss, we have nowhere else to turn. It is at that moment that our eyes are opened to the one great truth: "Not I, but Christ." We can't do it ourselves, but "with God all things are possible." When we finally comprehend and embrace that truth, everything changes.

THERE IS a Visa commercial that has a tag line that says, "Life comes at you pretty fast." I can honestly say that life moves pretty fast, especially when you are going through a difficult time. It seems like the events that I just described were moving at least a hundred miles per hour. As quickly as one reality occurred, another one was fast approaching on the horizon. Challenges and difficulties seem to rush upon us, not giving us very much time to adjust or to process what is happening.

That is why we need to have some bedrock principles from the Word of God for the foundation of our lives. I probably had read Galatians 2:20 ("I am crucified with Christ: nevertheless I live; yet not I, but Christ liveth in me," KJV) a hundred times before, but this time I wasn't reading it for inspiration, I was leaning on it for survival. "Not I, but Christ" was no longer a verse in the Bible, it was a principle for my life. Hopefully, you have also come to the place that Christ is not just a comforting thought or a heartwarming idea, but a way of life.

QUESTIONS TO CONSIDER

1. When did Christ become more than just a word or an idea in your life?
2. What does "Not I, but Christ" mean to you?
3. How can you apply this simple prayer today?: "Lord, I can't do it, but you can. So please, do it. Amen."

UPWARD LOOK:

Dear God, thank you for the promises that you have given to me in your Word. Help me to realize that "not I, but Christ" is a principle that will change my way of thinking, acting, and living. Thank you for loving me and sending your Son to die not only for my sins, but for the sins of the entire world. I believe Jesus died on the cross for me and I ask Jesus to come into my life and take control of my life. In Jesus' name, amen.

3

Not My Sufficiency, but Christ's

As I WALKED onto the platform that first Sunday morning following Dad's death, I knew how completely incapable I was of stepping into the shoes of my father. But there was no turning back. Face-to-face with the crowd that had filled the room, I couldn't simply walk back off the stage as if I had never arrived. My pulse quickened until I was certain those standing near me could hear my thunderous heartbeat. Though I had found freedom in the great biblical truth of "Not I, but Christ," I still felt the seemingly inescapable weight of my own inadequacy bearing down on me.

The service began, music seeming to bring with it the very presence of God as our three-hundred-voice choir sang "The Days of

Elijah." Their voices swelled and filled the room like I had never heard before. I actually turned around to see if the group had grown by great numbers since the previous week, because it sounded like many more voices than I remembered.

As the song rang out with the comforting words about the power of God, I walked to my seat and looked out at the faces of many people I had come to know and appreciate through the years. I scanned the room to get a feel for the spirit of the audience. A few people were attempting to put up a strong front, but their emotions were betraying them. Everywhere I looked, I saw expressions of grief. Their dearly loved pastor of nearly fifty-one years was gone, and their hearts were breaking.

One elderly couple on the front row had tears flowing down their faces. The husband pulled his wife close to him in an attempt to comfort her as she wept, shaking in her anguish. Soon the husband also began to shudder as he was overcome with emotion.

In another section a young woman was wiping her eyes with a tissue. She tried to stop the tears, but they were irrepressible. She reached into her purse to find more tissues. Next to her was a long-time member of the church who had always been close to Dad. He was biting his lip, trying to be strong, but it was a losing battle. Uncharacteristically, he reached into his coat pocket and pulled out a travel-size pack of tissues. You normally wouldn't find this man with a pocket full of Kleenex, but today was far from normal.

Back in the choir loft, all three hundred members were wearing tributes to Dad on their collars. Dad was known to wear, almost exclusively, black suits. He and Johnny Cash probably had more black clothes in their closets than anyone else I've ever met. Dad also typically wore a red (or some shade of red) tie. And on his lapel he always wore a gold Jesus First pin. He had these pins designed in 1977 and began giving them away through our church's television ministry. Over the past thirty years, he had given away more than ten million of those pins. He never walked out of the house without that pin proudly displayed.

In tribute to Dad, the choir—and many people in the audience—were wearing little black ribbons (representing his suits) that had red ribbons (folded like neckties) running down the middle, set off with Jesus First pins. What a thoughtful way for Dad's friends to pay their respects to him and to honor his passion for serving Christ. And every single member of the choir wore one proudly. As they sang, lifting their voices in praise to God, I could see that many were having a difficult time. Tears flowed freely even as they sang with all their hearts. Some looked down and smiled at me, even through tears. Several flashed a thumbs-up sign to reassure me that everything would be fine. I wanted to believe them, but I wasn't so sure.

While I certainly understood the tears that were flowing that morning, these were not the sights I needed to see as I tried desperately to steel myself to stand on that platform and speak.

It was nine o'clock. This was the early service, as we call it, and attendance is usually somewhat lower than in our eleven o'clock service. But that day the sanctuary was filled with a capacity crowd of about 5,500 people. Members and visitors from across Central Virginia had come to church to find comfort. I couldn't help feeling that I was the one who needed to be comforted. Yet I knew that the job of comforter fell on my shoulders that day.

The presence of the Holy Spirit was almost palpable as people joined their hearts together to praise God, even in the midst of their sorrow. And I felt a wrenching in my stomach. Seven days earlier, Dad had stood in the very place I was now standing. I looked at the small wooden desk that sat next to the chair where my Bible was resting. Just seven days earlier, Dad's Bible had rested there. Only seven days ago Dad was about to stand in the same pulpit I was preparing to approach. I could focus on nothing but the crushing loss.

I fought back tears. Someone had placed a box of tissues beside my chair that morning, and I reached down and grabbed several to put in my pocket in case I needed them once I started to speak. I didn't want to show weakness. I didn't want people to see my tears. I felt that I needed to be strong for them. But it was even more diffi-cult than I had anticipated.

Again I wrestled with my thoughts: *I don't have what it takes to stand in my father's pulpit. I'm unqualified to encourage this congrega-tion. I'm not capable of leading this church into the future.* My mind became my worst enemy as these doubts raged and rendered me vir-tually helpless as I waited to begin my sermon. And suddenly it was time.

I stepped up to the pulpit and opened my Bible to Joshua chap-ter 1. I looked across the room for a moment, then began sharing truths from that book. I shared how God had promised Joshua and the entire nation of Israel that he would supply all of their needs. I shared the promises God had given to his people thousands of years ago as if those promises were aimed directly at those sitting in front of me. And the words sank deep into my own heart as well. I found a freedom to speak that was, without doubt, a blessing from God. It seemed those words were tailor-made for the situation we were now facing.

As I came to the end of the sermon, I read what Spurgeon's son had so eloquently said about his father. And as I shared those final four words, "Not I, but Christ," I offered to the thousands in that room the same promise that had already comforted me and that would, in the days to come, change the lives of many others. In our weakness, Christ is strong. In our mourning, Christ brings joy. In our loss, Christ will be our all. In our doubt, Christ is steadfast.

The service ended with thousands of people gathering at the altar for a time of personal prayer. As I knelt beside my dad's chair on that platform, Shari and our four children—Jonathan Jr., Jessica, Natalie, and Nicholas—joined me. The kids all told me they loved me. Shari gently kissed me and told me how proud she was of the job I had done. Yet I firmly understood that I had done nothing. God had done it all.

The power we all felt in the room that day would be the power that would propel us to continue the mission of our church. And the words "Not I, but Christ" became the message that not only bolstered our spirits that day but has empowered us in our weakness ever since.

In 2 Corinthians the apostle Paul sheds further light on what those four words from Galatians 2:20 truly mean: "He [the Lord] said, 'My grace is all you need. My power works best in weakness.' So now I am glad to boast about my weaknesses, so that the power of Christ can work through me" (2 Corinthians 12:9).

One truth that is evident in the life of Joshua is his utter dependence on God as the only source of his strength. It's what made him a great leader. It's what can make us great too. We must come to understand that our weakness is actually a powerful tool. I imagine this doesn't make sense to some of you, so let me expound. You see, when we identify our weakness, we're able to, in a way, embrace that weakness. And by doing so, we see our need. At that point we can begin to see the true power of God. In our weaknesses, we find the opportunity to allow him to move in ways we could never imagine. I believe that this is one of the great truths of the Bible that can transform us into the people God has designed us to be. In weakness, we can triumph if we allow Christ to work through us.

As I said, in order for us to be able to embrace this truth, we must be willing to embrace our weakness. This, however, might be substantially more difficult than we are willing to acknowledge. Typically, human nature wants to avoid any admission, any appearance, of weakness. We're more often than not driven by our own desires to be winners. But for us to truly tap in to God's power, we must be able to identify and then accept our weakness. And we must be able to acknowledge that this weakness is impossible to overcome unless we allow God to take charge. This, however, is easier said than done because of a common condition we all face at some point in our lives: pride.

In my senior year of high school, a friend encouraged me to try out for the baseball team. I had never played baseball. I didn't even know many of the rules of the game. I'd never watched baseball on television or attended games in person. The truth of the matter was, I'd never had any interest in the game. But I was actually considering trying out. My friend Andy and I began practicing each day after school. He was an accomplished athlete who had played baseball most of his life and had a bright future in the game. He was already talking to colleges about scholarship opportunities. I, on the other hand, was still trying to figure out the game.

Each day as we threw the ball back and forth, I started to get a handle on the nuances of baseball. Andy continued teaching me and felt that I had enough ability to try out for the team. By the first day of tryouts, I was ready to give it a shot. I walked into the batting cage, put on the batting helmet, grabbed a bat, and signaled that I was ready to swing away. Andy fed balls into a ball machine at the other end of the cage. The first ball flew toward me, and I swung. *Whack!* Not bad. I dug in for the next pitch. *Whack!* I was off to a great start. I hit each ball that was sent my way, and at the end of the tryout that day, I had hit more consecutive balls than any other person there. I was pretty impressed with myself, and I wasn't afraid to let everyone know how well I had done.

As we left, Andy noted that hitting balls inside the cage was one thing, but hitting them out on the field with a live pitcher was quite different. But after my stellar showing in the cage, I felt like I had it all under control. In fact, I made the team, started practicing regularly, and started to believe I was really something.

After several weeks of intense practice, it was time for our first game. I stepped confidently to the plate, certain I would get a hit in my first at bat.

Here's what actually happened.

First pitch. Swing and a miss. Second pitch. Swing and a miss. Third pitch. You guessed it: I flailed futilely at the third pitch and was down on strikes. *Oh well,* I thought, *it was probably just first-time jitters.* A few days later I was anxious to face another pitcher in game action. Yet again I struck out in my first two at bats. *Okay,* I thought, *something isn't right here.* I reminded myself that I was the guy who had hit more balls in the batting cage than anyone else. Something had gone miserably wrong since that day, so I asked Andy why I was failing. He reminded me of his comments that first day: it's not the same when you face a live pitcher as it is in the batting cage. We kept practicing, and I started to regain a little confidence. When my turn at bat came during the next game, I walked to the plate with renewed determination. And in that first at bat, I struck out again.

The season progressed, but my game didn't. I wasn't giving up, though. The more strikeouts I had, the more committed I became to figuring out how to get a hit. Finally it was time for a big game in our city's historic professional stadium, where the Lynchburg Hillcats (a minor league team of the Pittsburgh Pirates) play their games. To say I was nervous would be an understatement. My parents were in the stands, and lots of friends and classmates had come out to watch the game as well.

The time came for me to step up to the plate. I ambled into the batter's box, fully anticipating failure and embarrassment, but willing to go through the motions. I looked out at the pitcher's mound and watched my opponent go into his windup. On the first pitch I swung, and to my great surprise, I heard a not-too-familiar sound: *whack!* I had actually hit the ball. It flew out toward center field, and I ran with all my might while watching the ball fall in front of the center fielder. I had a single. I could hardly believe it. I was thrilled that I had finally found success on the baseball diamond and that my friends and family were there to see it. With a huge grin on my face, I looked back into the stands and found the smiling faces of Mom and Dad. Dad was on his feet clapping and cheering. I had finally done something right on the field.

Remember, now, that this was my first hit of the entire season. I wasn't used to standing on first base or running the bases or being aware of what was taking place on the field around me. And so, in my celebration of that first hit, I forgot to focus on the fact that the pitcher might try to pick me off at first base. As I took a few steps leading off of the bag, I simply was not paying attention to him when he threw the ball to the first baseman. I tried to skip back to first, but the first baseman nabbed the throw and slapped it on me. The umpire blared, "You're out!" The smile on my face swiftly disappeared. My success had suddenly turned to abject failure. I walked back to the dugout in anger and shame. My first hit of the season had been wasted because I hadn't paid attention to the game.

Here's the point I want to make with this story. After that first day of baseball tryouts, I thought I had it all together because I'd been able to hit the ball so easily. I even entertained thoughts that I might have some untapped talent and that maybe I would turn out to be a baseball star, just like my father had been in high school. Even through all of the strikeouts in those first few games, I still believed I had talent. The truth was that in order for me to really develop, I needed to admit my limitation. And my limitation was that I had no real talent for baseball.

Life is not much different from the story of my failed high school baseball career. You see, our human nature often compels us to believe that we're greater than we really are. We achieve some rudimentary success, and suddenly we think we're special. We believe that we are far more capable, far more intelligent, and far more important than we really are. The reality is that we are almost always less capable, less intelligent, and certainly much less important than we think we are. And when we believe our own lies that convince us of our great importance, we are headed for failure.

If Joshua had been convinced of his own strength and ability when it came time to step into Moses' shoes, he undoubtedly would have struck out as a leader. The job was just too big for anyone to handle alone. But Joshua didn't have to. He clearly saw his own insufficiency and turned to the One who could make him strong and help him succeed. So what does Joshua's example teach us about preparing to lead God's way?

Depend on God's Presence

WE CANNOT allow our problems or feelings of inadequacy to prevent our service to God. When personal trials or doubts come into our lives, we must cling to God's promise in Joshua 1:9—"Be strong and courageous! Do not be afraid or discouraged. For the LORD your God is with you wherever you go." There, in a clear and concise statement, God promises that he will be with us no matter where we are. When everything goes wrong in life, he will be there. When we feel like we have nowhere to turn and nowhere to go to escape our problems, he will be there. That's God's great promise, and it's one I've seen him keep so wondrously in my own life.

We all want to be successful. We all want to make a difference in life, regardless of the career path we've chosen. Yet many times we don't give ourselves the opportunity to succeed because we think we're walking through life alone. Even many believers who understand that God is available to help them through the challenges of life often choose not to accept his outstretched hand and embrace the power of Christ in their lives.

I may never understand why God took Dad when he did, but I can go on, even in my despair. And while this may not make the grief any easier to bear, it does make the road ahead more bearable because I know that I'm not walking it alone.

Moses died. Jerry Falwell died. Many great Christian men and women who have inspired us have died and gone on to the reward God has for his children in heaven. We remain. Our efforts for Christ go on, and they should go on with undiminished enthusiasm. New hands must take on new roles. We all can be willing to step into these new roles—roles that may initially seem overwhelming—because our great and perfect God is with us wherever we go. When we stand on God's promises, we simply cannot fail. And when we face a daunting reality in our lives and feel that we just can't handle it alone, we can trust that we really aren't alone at all. God is there.

He was there for Moses. He was there for Joshua. He was there for Jerry Falwell. He's been there for me in ways I can't even begin to explain in this book. And he is there for you.

Depend on God's Sufficiency

AS WE sat in that church auditorium just a few days after our Moses had died, we were looking for many answers. We were looking for some direction for how to go on. We, like the children of Israel, were standing out in our proverbial wilderness not knowing where to go next. And those words in the first chapter of Joshua were exactly what we needed to hear. I told our congregation that this message that God gave Joshua was the same message he was giving to us following the death of our leader.

The mandate was given by God, and it is our responsibility, our challenge, to carry on the heaven-inspired vision of Jerry Falwell in our church. Just as the children of Israel would not quit simply because Moses had gone on to be with the Lord, Thomas Road Baptist Church would carry on, undaunted, in the light of God's direction. That was the message God had for Joshua, and it was the message God had for me. And I can assure you, it's the message God has for everyone facing a challenge.

You may not feel adequate for the task before you, but God is more than adequate. Recognize that it doesn't depend on you but on God. Admit your limitations, embrace your weakness, and depend on God to work in and through you. With God's help, you can conquer all the new territory he wants to give you. As he told Joshua: " 'Wherever you set foot, you will be on land I have given you. . . .' No one will be able to stand against you as long as you live. For I will be with you as I was with Moses" (Joshua 1:3–5).

We can succeed in anything to which God has called us, for God has promised to be with us—preparing the way, helping us, and fighting the battle for us. But along with this great promise comes responsibility. You see, the promises God gave to Joshua and the children of Israel were not simply offered without requiring anything on their part.

We can't take to heart the comforting words of Joshua chapter 1 without also taking to heart the commands God gave to Joshua: "Be careful to obey all the instructions Moses gave you. Do not deviate from them, turning either to the right or to the left. Then you will be successful in everything you do. Study this Book of Instruction continually. Meditate on it day and night so you will be sure to obey everything written in it. Only then will you prosper and succeed in all you do" (verses 7–8).

Did you catch that? God has given us the keys to success in leadership and life. Let's look at those a little more closely.

Key 1: We Must Obey God's Laws

IN THE months since taking on the leadership role at Thomas Road, I have seen anew how our relationship with Christ requires something of us. We cannot expect a one-sided relationship with God for our own convenience. It cannot be a casual relationship or one that is occasional or inspired by a sudden, urgent need in our lives. Our relationship with God must be enduring and unswerving. We must live our lives firmly committed to personal holiness and doing everything we can to reflect Christ in our lives.

Key 2: We Must Study God's Word

WE MUST be committed to God's Word and steep ourselves in the Bible so that God can continually reveal himself to us. Remember that God has promised that if we meditate on his Word, this will prevent us from going in the wrong direction (see Psalm 119:105). When we depart from God's Word, we tend to drift all over the place in our lives.

Key 3: We Must Pray

WE MUST be committed to prayer. My father often said, "Nothing of eternal importance is ever accomplished apart from prayer." We have to learn that when we are on our knees before God, our hearts become tender and open to God's touch. My dad also often said that "all of our failures are nothing more than prayer failures." You see, just as Moses encountered God in that burning bush, and just as Joshua heard the voice of God, so we must hear God's message to us. Prayer is a conversation we have with the Almighty. There are times when we feel alone and cannot feel the presence of God in our hearts. That's because we're human. But especially at those times, through prayer, we can know that we are never really alone; God is always with us. We must be willing to enter into that conversation with him at every turn of life—not just when we face our Jordan.

Key 4: Just Do It!

GOD CALLED Joshua to lead the people of Israel into the Promised Land. That was the way Joshua was to serve God. Joshua didn't overthink this or wallow in his own insufficiencies; he simply stepped out in faith and did what God commanded. We, too, must be committed to God's service. We are called, just as Joshua was thousands of years ago, to cross the river to the land he has promised us. We are called by God to serve him, to bring him glory in all that we do. As Rick Warren so poignantly explained in his book *The Purpose Driven® Life,* it's not about us; it's always about God.

We are called to reach out to this lost and dying world with the gospel, to preach that message unashamedly, to preach it compassionately, and to preach it continually. We must always be ready to show the world the power that comes from God and the love that only he can give.

Why are these things so important? Why must we look to God to guide our lives instead of looking within? As Joshua 1:8 explains it, "Only then will you prosper and succeed in all you do." Who doesn't want to prosper and succeed?

By following these principles, we'll find unspeakable fulfillment. Whether in our careers, our families, or our faith, we all want fulfillment. I'm not talking about the earthly fulfillment we often talk about in modern society. This world has a skewed perspective of fulfillment. We live in a culture where everyone wants immediate satisfaction, usually in the form of quick and cheap gratification that has no enduring value.

As Christians, we have other options. We will be able to do what God has called us to do because of his great power within us. And when we carry out God's call on our lives, we find true fulfillment. Even more, beyond ourselves, we'll see lives changed and souls saved as a result of God's great power within us.

NOT LONG ago I received an email from a young man who had just been accepted by a church as its senior pastor. This was his first time serving in such a role, and he shared his nervousness with me. He said that while he knew God had called him to be a minister, he felt as if he had no clue what to do. As I read this email, a smile spread across my face. I told him not to worry—I commonly feel as if I have no clue. I added that this is exactly the place God likes us to be, in ministry and in life. It is when we realize our own imperfection and weakness that we can finally see the one great truth. When we understand that we're incapable of achieving meaningful success by our own power, we are driven to depend on someone else to help us. That someone must always be the God of the universe.

Knowing that God works through our often-clueless selves is a wonderful thing. The freedom and joy it brings cannot be replicated by any purchase we make or any accomplishment we can realize on our own. Once again we see that real success—and true fulfillment—can only come from knowing that it is "Not I, but Christ."

WHAT IS the most embarrassing thing that has ever happened to you? Striking out at home plate? Falling down in front of a crowd? Losing your place in a speech? I could go on, because there are a lot of opportunities for embarrassment. It is a target-rich environment. Sometimes failure is God's reminder that pride has crept into our lives. Depending on God's presence and on God's sufficiency are good ways to avoid the trap of pride.

If we are leaving God out of our lives, we are basically telling God that we can handle this life on our own terms. That is not a good message to send to the creator God. That is like preschoolers telling parents that they no longer need their help and that from now on they can handle life on their own. Ridiculous, isn't it? That's how we must sound to God when we leave him out of our lives, either consciously or subconsciously. The end result is that we don't have time for God. No time for God means we are under the grip and spell of pride.

The Bible tells us that pride comes before a fall (see Proverbs 16:8 NLV). To avoid an embarrassing fall, confess your sin and return to Christ. Invest time in prayer and Bible study, and before long, "Not I, but Christ" will be not just a motto or a phrase; it will be a way of life.

QUESTIONS TO CONSIDER

1. We all know the phrase, "three strikes and you're out!" What have you put a lot of heart and soul into, but still struck out at?

2. As a general rule of life, pride leads to heartache. What are some areas of your life where pride is hurting your potential impact?

3. How can the principle, "Not I, but Christ" help you avoid the pitfall of pride?

UPWARD LOOK:

Dear God, thank you for helping me to realize that pride leads to heartache. I ask that you will help me to lean on You for my sufficiency in times of trial and in my everyday life. I realize that Christ is what I need and He is all I need. I commit my will and my future to Christ. In Jesus' name, amen.

4

Not My Plan, but God's

WHEN DAD DIED, the plans and timeline I had for my own life were shattered. I didn't know what each new day might bring, much less how I could possibly accomplish all that would need to be done. But I soon was reminded that it wasn't about me and my plans, but about God and his plans. "Not I, but Christ." I didn't need to know everything or see how it all fit together—how I fit into God's plan—in those days and weeks after Dad's death. I only needed to trust God, knowing that he doesn't make mistakes. As much as I couldn't, and still don't, understand why God chose to take my father when he still had so much to offer, I know that God has a plan. And I trust that God's plan is a perfect plan for my life, for the lives of my family, and for God's ministry through us.

In the months since Dad's death, I have seen glimpses of God's plan for our church. Thousands of people have since come to know Christ and his power in their lives. God's way of revealing his power in our lives sometimes takes unexpected turns and brings us to a place of unforeseen challenges.

Our response to these challenges is what defines us. We have a choice at these pivotal times in our lives: (1) we can retreat within ourselves and let grief overwhelm us and prevent us from feeling God's tender touch, or (2) we can allow God to carry us to greater heights as a result of the suffering we experience.

When I was faced with the reality that my dad was gone, I had to choose how I would carry on from that day forward. I could have decided to live in the past, to dwell on all the amazing things I had learned and experienced watching my dad over the past forty-one years, and spend the rest of my days looking back. Or I could choose to build on those experiences, reflecting on the value of those times but looking forward and allowing them to be building blocks for the future. These two options are not unique to my situation. They are basically true in the lives of every individual. We must choose between these two paths on a regular basis.

Many, unfortunately, choose to live in the past. I've seen many people throughout my years of ministry who cling so tightly to their precious memories that they become like shackles around their ankles. It is not, however, the memories themselves that hold us down. It is our tendency to let those memories keep us from looking forward. This is where so many get bogged down in defeat. Living in the past can never be a path to success. A person who wallows in his or her sorrow will never make it out into a life of victory.

When I finally hit that baseball in my senior year of high school and made it to first base, I was thrilled. Yet the defeat I felt moments later when the pitcher picked me off was, at first, overwhelming. After all that time, I finally got a hit, and it had to end that way . . . and in front of so many people. I was fuming. I stormed back toward the dugout, yanked off my helmet, and threw it in the direction of the dugout in disgust. It flew for several feet, bounced off the dirt in front of the dugout, and slammed against the back wall. I stalked past several teammates without saying a word and dropped onto the bench, hidden from the crowd. No one said a word to me; they didn't even look my way.

Moments later my dad came around the corner of the dugout and walked over to where I was sitting. I was certain he would sympathize with what I'd just been through. Surely my dad was furious that the pitcher had the audacity to throw that ball to first base when I wasn't looking. I was angry, and I knew Dad would be angry too.

Indeed, I was correct. But Dad wasn't mad at the pitcher or the first baseman. He wasn't mad that I'd been picked off because I was standing too far from the base, ready to rush to second. He wasn't mad that I'd been embarrassed in front of so many people. He was mad *at me*.

As I looked up at him, I quickly felt the wrath of his visit to the dugout. He didn't yell. He really didn't even raise his voice. He simply looked down at me and said, "Son, don't you ever throw your helmet again. You will not be a whiner. You get out there when it's your turn at bat, and you start over and don't act like that again."

We all face times of anger, grief, pain, and distress. We all have times in our lives when we want to throw our proverbial helmets into the dirt and hide in humiliation. We want to sulk when we've been wronged, when we've been treated badly or unfairly. Or when dealt a life-changing blow . . . such as the death of a loved one.

We desperately want to tuck ourselves away in the dugouts of life, out of sight of the crowds, where we can indulge in self-loathing, pity, and anger. Unfortunately, when we go to that place, we rarely come out quickly. We usually end up staying for a long time. And during that time, little or nothing of value can come from our lives. We can't move forward when we're locked in self-pity.

In the course of our lives, sometimes we need a fresh start. A time when we can simply lay aside where we are and what we've been doing so that we can begin anew. Sometimes, while we may be acutely aware that this is necessary, we aren't quite ready to make this commitment. Most of the time, however, we really have no other choice. This is where I found myself on May 15, 2007. I knew I needed to get back to the basics in order to find direction for the future. That's easy to talk about; it's far more difficult to put into practice. Yet in order to begin living the freedom of the one great truth, we must be willing to start fresh.

As I shared on that first Sunday after Dad's death, Joshua found himself in a similar situation. After the death of Moses, Joshua must have wondered how it would be possible to move forward. Yet God told Joshua to do just that: get up and march forward.

Joshua had led the army in battle (see Exodus 17:9–14); he was Moses' assistant (from his youth—see Numbers 11:28), climbing the mountain of God with Moses when God gave him the Ten Commandments (see Exodus 24); he was with Moses in the Tent of Meeting when Moses met with God, and remained behind in the tent when Moses returned to the people (see Exodus 33:10–12); he was one of the spies sent to scout out the Promised Land who stood up against the people and popular opinion, declaring that with God's help they could take the land (see Numbers 13 and 14); and he was loyal to Moses and supportive of his leadership (see Numbers 11:27–29). He saw that God was with Moses. He knew the relationship was unparalleled and would never again be equaled (see Deuter-onomy 34:10). Now God asked Joshua to move forward without Moses and assume the responsibility Moses had shouldered.

Listen to the words God said to Joshua: "Moses my servant is dead. Therefore, the time has come for you to lead these people, the Israelites, across the Jordan River into the land I am giving them" (Joshua 1:2). General Charles De Gaulle once said, "The graveyards are full of indispensable men." Men of great importance are often deemed to be without equal. But when they die, someone must step into their shoes; someone always does.

I'm sure the children of Israel saw Moses as being irreplaceable. I'm sure that when Moses drew his last breath, the people worried: now what? Remember, they were out in the wilderness. Moses had been used by God to deliver them from the hands of the Egyptians, but they still needed guidance and help to take possession of the Promised Land. And their leader was no longer in front, showing them the way.

But God had prepared Joshua for the task of replacing Moses. It's important to note that God never fails to equip us for the roles he has for us to play. He's not going to throw us into the fires of minis-try unprepared and alone.

Regardless of what Joshua may have been feeling personally, he didn't hesitate to obey God. When God said to move, Joshua moved. "Joshua then commanded the officers of Israel, 'Go through the camp and tell the people to get their provisions ready. In three days you will cross the Jordan River and take possession of the land the LORD your God is giving you' " (Joshua 1:10–11). Joshua didn't sulk in the midst of uncertainty and pain. He took God at his word. He told the Israelites to get ready, because God wasn't finished with them yet. The nation was facing a transformation; they had no choice about that. Moses was gone . . . change was upon them. Their choice rested in how to respond and chart a course for the future. They really only had two options: go forward or go nowhere. Only one option would lead them to victory. Joshua chose the former.

I believe that in many ways we are all, at times, just like Joshua. We all have special roles that God wants us to fill throughout the course of our lives. It's seldom possible to accomplish the tasks God has for us or to assume the next big role without change. Facing transformations in life is natural. It's also unavoidable. My life had been fairly routine and free of unwelcome change for forty years. And then, upon my father's death, I faced days more traumatic than any I'd ever known. Dad was gone, and I had suddenly become the pastor of a twenty-one-thousand-member church whose people were looking to me for solace and wisdom.

In response to this dramatic change in my life, I began contemplating Bible characters who had been suddenly thrust into new roles and given heavy responsibilities. I began to focus on how God ministered to these individuals. While Joshua became the biblical character with whom I most identified, I found several other figures whose stories encouraged me and roused my spirit. People like . . .

Joseph, the man engaged to Mary. His simple, well-ordered life was turned upside down through no choice or fault of his own when he learned his betrothed was pregnant—and the child certainly was not his. Joseph was troubled, as any man would be, by this revelation and the implication that Mary had been unfaithful to him. Now, what Joseph could only assume was Mary's moral failing had left them both open to scorn, loss of social standing and opportunity, and harsh judgment. No matter what course of action Joseph chose, his life was changing dramatically in a way he had never dreamed or sought. But even when thrust into this potentially devastating situation that would have led many men to simply walk away, Joseph remained a man of character and great faith.

It's tempting to want to just walk away from our problems, especially when we face situations that change our lives through no fault or action of our own. But just imagine how a negative reaction from Joseph would have altered the entire story of Jesus' birth. Instead of thinking only of what was good for himself and turning his back on Mary, Joseph came to understand that he had an important role to play in God's plan in sending his Son to be born of a virgin, Mary, Joseph's betrothed. He became a willing vessel even though he knew there would be whispers and false accusations about Mary and about him. And because of his steadfastness, Joseph came to comprehend that he would play a key role in God's plan for mankind. He was there to experience the divine birth of the Savior and to help raise this extraordinary gift from heaven.

We must be willing to look beyond the immediacy of our difficulties so that God can work in our lives and bring honor to himself. God greatly blessed Joseph for his faithfulness. Joseph was accorded the extraordinary responsibility of being the earthly father of Jesus. This is a picture of how, when we turn to God instead of looking inward or acting without thinking, God can work for his glory in our lives, even in the most trying situations.

Joseph, son of Jacob. Joseph was a much-loved eleventh son of a wealthy patriarch with twelve sons. As a young man, he had dreams that hinted at greatness and being elevated above his family members. His life path seemed secure and favorable. But his jealous older brothers changed all that, selling Joseph into slavery and placing him in just about the worst situation imaginable. Joseph became a slave in the house of Potiphar, the captain of Pharaoh's guard. We read in Genesis that the Lord blessed Potiphar's house simply because Joseph was there. Things were turning around for Joseph. But then Joseph was slammed down hard again. Potiphar's wife turned her affections toward him and tried to seduce Joseph. And even though he resisted the lure of this woman day after day, Joseph was in big trouble. Unhappy with his continuing rebuffs, Potiphar's wife falsely accused Joseph of attempted rape; and in a rage, Potiphar had Joseph thrown into jail for a crime he hadn't committed.

It's important to learn this now: just because you live an honorable, godly life and prayerfully walk with God to the best of your ability does not mean that tough times will not come your way. Even though Joseph was upright, Potiphar's wife was able to convince her husband that it was Joseph, not she, who had been making illicit advances. And he was swept off to prison. Yet even there, seemingly forgotten by God while incarcerated, Joseph's faith would not be dampened. Shortly after this darkest of times, God blessed Joseph. Ultimately he became a ruler of Egypt and a striking example of forgiveness to the brothers who had betrayed him.

It was after the birth of his second son that Joseph made a wonderful statement: "God has made me fruitful in this land of my grief" (Genesis 41:52). Even when we are faced with dire afflictions and hardships, God is at work in our lives. We must embody the principle "Not I, but Christ," letting God work through us just as Joseph did. When we can fully and selflessly embrace this concept in our lives, we, too, will be fruitful even in the land of our grief.

Gideon. At a time when Israel was impoverished and in bondage to the Midianites, God looked down on an unsuspecting young man who was threshing wheat and chose him to deliver Israel from its affliction. In fact, God called this unlikeliest of heroes a "mighty hero" (Judges 6:12).

Gideon initially thought the Lord had the wrong man, saying,

"How can I rescue Israel? My clan is the weakest in the whole tribe of Manasseh, and I am the least in my entire family!" (Judges 6:15). I'm sure we've all felt inadequate when God leads us down new paths or brings new challenges into our lives. I can certainly see elements of myself in Gideon. Following Dad's death, I had similar thoughts about leading Thomas Road Baptist Church. *Surely,* I thought, *there must be someone more prepared to take on such a task.* Yet even in my inadequacy, God has richly blessed our church. We have seen that God's ways are always perfect, and as I earlier noted, he will not place us in situations without properly equipping us.

We may not even realize that God has equipped us until we're cast into the storm and we see him wondrously working in our lives. Gideon had no idea that he could lead the armies of God until he was called into duty. Seeing how God used Gideon to defeat the enemies of Israel, we learn that he also will use us when we surrender our lives to his perfect will.

Abraham and Isaac. Isaac was the promised son of Abraham and Sarah, born to the couple in their old age because of God's providence, and the fulfillment of God's covenant with Israel. But the Bible tells us that God tested Abraham by charging him to do the following: "Take your son, your only son—yes, Isaac, whom you love so much—and go to the land of Moriah. Go and sacrifice him as a burnt offering on one of the mountains, which I will show you" (Genesis 22:2). It's hard to fathom the feeling Abraham must have had after receiving these instructions from God. But he obeyed.

And Isaac, foreshadowing the Savior, bore the wood upon his back as he and his father, who carried the fire, traveled up the mountain. As the two walked on, Isaac asked his father, "We have the fire and the wood . . . but where is the sheep for the burnt offering?"

(Genesis 22:7). And in verse 8 Abraham responded with words we must all carry in our hearts: "God will provide." Even when we walk up our own mountains of doubt, we must be willing to let God work in our lives. Notice that Abraham didn't bargain with God or try to find solutions apart from God's will. Abraham personified the New Testament tenet "Not I, but Christ."

We see also that Isaac was a willing sacrifice. After the father and son had arrived at their destination and the wood was prepared, the boy was bound and placed on the alter. Only when Abraham raised the knife to sacrifice his only son did God cry out from heaven, "Don't lay a hand on the boy! . . . Do not hurt him in any way, for now I know that you truly fear God. You have not withheld from me even your son, your only son" (Genesis 22:12). When Abraham looked up, he saw a ram in the thicket. God had provided. Even today, God may put us through tests and allow hardships to come our way. But when we willingly allow him to work in our hearts without complaining or negotiating, we, like Abraham and Isaac, can experience the miraculous in our lives.

The apostle Paul. Throughout his ministry, Paul faced incredible, often life-threatening challenges. In the book of Acts we read of Paul's stirring defense of the faith to throngs of Jews and Gentiles. He appeared before a Roman court, addressing the Sanhedrin and preaching to King Agrippa. He used these situations to glorify God.

In Acts 16 we're told that some local religious leaders incited a crowd against Paul and Silas, who were accused of causing an "uproar." A local magistrate had the two stripped and beaten. Later they were thrown into prison and placed in stocks. The situation couldn't have been much worse. So what did Paul and Silas do? "Around midnight Paul and Silas were praying and singing hymns to

God, and the other prisoners were listening" (verse 25). When you're in dire straits, don't forget or abandon God—because he has neither forgotten nor abandoned you. Here's what happened next:

> Suddenly, there was a massive earthquake, and the prison was shaken to its foundations. All the doors immediately flew open, and the chains of every prisoner fell off! The jailer woke up to see the prison doors wide open. He assumed the prisoners had escaped, so he drew his sword to kill himself. But Paul shouted to him, "Stop! Don't kill yourself! We are all here!"
>
> The jailer called for lights and ran to the dungeon and fell down trembling before Paul and Silas. Then he brought them out and asked, "Sirs, what must I do to be saved?"
>
> They replied, "Believe in the Lord Jesus and you will be saved, along with everyone in your household." And they shared the word of the Lord with him and with all who lived in his household. (verses 26–32)

The jailer and his family were gloriously saved that night. They had witnessed how Paul and Silas praised God even when all hope seemed lost. If those men had been singing the blues instead of singing praises, this series of miracles and the salvation of this family might never have happened.

We must not allow the chains of our circumstances to bind us and prevent us from wholly trusting God. It is then that we will see miraculous events unfold in our lives and in the lives of people near and dear to us. We must learn to praise God even when the trials of life are heavy upon our shoulders.

Has life led you down unexpected paths? Are you facing unanticipated trials? Does all seem hopeless?

Then immerse yourself in God's Word. When we walk down new and possibly dark corridors of life, may we remember the words of Psalm 119:105—"Your word is a lamp to guide my feet and a light for my path."

The Bible has a way of cutting to the heart of our circumstances. We need to read the Bible daily, of course. But when we face trials or loss or new challenges, we must more keenly focus on the Scriptures. Relive these and other wonderful stories to see how God fulfills his promises to his children, and be encouraged in knowing that he remains the true and living God who is miraculously at work in each of our lives.

The two Josephs, Gideon, Abraham and Isaac, and Paul were ordinary people—flawed individuals, like the rest of us—who were extraordinarily used by God. He can do the same in your life, if you let him.

MANY TIMES we forget that Bible characters were just normal human beings like you and me. They had hopes and dreams and they had fears and tears. They got up in the morning and had a routine and rhythm in their daily life, until something came along and brought them face to face with a challenge. They had a choice to make at the time of the challenge: lean on God and rise to meet the challenge with God or lean on their own resources and fail. The two Josephs, Gideon, Abraham and Isaac, and Paul were ordinary people—flawed individuals like the rest of us—who were extraordinarily used by God. They made the choice to follow God's will for their lives, and as a result they experienced "Not I, but Christ." He can do the same in your life, if you let him.

QUESTIONS TO CONSIDER

1. What big plans have you made that suddenly disappeared in an instant?
2. What emotions did you feel when the plan evaporated before your very eyes?
3. We have a choice at these pivotal times in our lives: (1) We can retreat within ourselves and let grief overwhelm us and prevent us from feeling God's tender touch; or (2) We can allow God to carry us to greater heights as a result of the suffering we experience. Which one will you choose?

UPWARD LOOK:

Dear God, thank you for giving us so many examples in the Bible. Thank you that the men and women in the Bible were just like me. I am grateful to understand I can overcome the trials in life just like they did as I keep my eyes on you. Help me to see trials as a way to grow and develop into your image. In Jesus' name, amen.

Not My Way, but God's

I N T H E D A Y S following my father's death, leading Thomas Road Baptist Church to the "promised land" of God's blessing made me feel as bewildered as Joshua must have felt as he stood facing the mighty Jordan River, swollen and angry at flood stage. Like Joshua, I knew the general direction God had called us to go, but how to actually get there was murky at best.

Following in the footsteps of a legend is difficult in the best of times, but having to cross a seemingly impassible barrier right off the bat hardly seems fair. If we had our way, life wouldn't be nearly so tough. If we had our way, we'd cross our rivers during the dry season or pray that God would send boats. But God's way often means crossing rivers at the absolute hardest time, humanly speaking. What kind of plan is that?

Our way seems better.

God's way is best.

Joshua discovered that, and so can you and I. It was harvest time in the land of Canaan as Joshua and the people approached the Jordan River, intent on crossing it. The river was overflowing its banks. The waters were rushing by and the current was strong. So much so that anyone who stepped into the waters could easily have been washed away. Can you imagine the scene that played itself out on that day? Joshua, the new leader of Israel, had led them right up to the banks of the Jordan, another body of water to cross. I have a feeling Joshua might have been quietly reevaluating his course of action. No, he didn't stand in front of the crowd and openly question whether he'd led them in the right direction. But I'll bet he had a few moments of soul-searching.

Is this what God wanted us to do? Are we heading in the right direction? Those questions are all too familiar in my own life. Many times I've found myself in essentially the same position as Joshua was that day. I recall several occasions when I arrived at a place I thought God wanted me to be, only to question whether it was of God at all.

One such time sticks out in my mind. Not long ago I was invited to attend a meeting in Washington DC with a number of ambassadors from Arab League nations. The purpose of this meeting was to discuss how evangelicals and Arabs could work together to bridge some pretty big divides between us. When I received the invitation, I was sitting in the office of Dr. Ron Godwin, executive vice president for administration at Liberty University. Ron had served alongside my dad for more than thirty years and was Dad's most trusted adviser outside of our family.

Ron and I discussed whether I should attend the meeting and how the outcome could affect what was happening at Thomas Road

Baptist Church. The meeting was scheduled to take place at the Egyptian embassy the morning after a large event at our church to commemorate Independence Day. More than twenty thousand people were expected to attend that evening service, and it wouldn't end until well after 11:00 p.m. due to the fireworks finale. I certainly didn't want to get up early the next morning and fly to Washington for a meeting that would, in my thinking, probably accomplish little.

After weighing several pros and cons, Ron said something that could only be described as prescient: "Jonathan, there's a reason you were invited to that meeting. I don't know what it is, but you should go. God may want you in that room." How could I argue with a statement like that? I said okay, with one condition: he had to go with me.

We boarded a plane early that Monday to fly to Washington. It was a beautiful morning, and as I looked out the window, I was impressed anew with God's creation. The sun was casting its red glow across the mountains as if an artist were painting this incredible scene and the paint was still wet. I was exhausted after the previous night's events. I had arrived home well after midnight, and it was much later before I got to sleep. I didn't feel like taking a trip this morning, but the view did make it a bit more bearable.

When we arrived at the Egyptian embassy, we were ushered into a large room where other evangelical leaders had already gathered. A few moments later a parade of Arab ambassadors entered. Ambassadors from Algeria, Morocco, Libya, Kuwait, Yemen, Iraq, Bahrain, and the Arab League of Nations joined the Egyptian ambassador, and we all moved to the adjacent dining room for lunch.

For several hours we ate, talked, and agreed to disagree on some important issues. I still wasn't sure what good had come from it and expressed to Ron my regret over our making the effort to attend. He simply smiled. During the meeting, I did have the chance to meet an evangelical leader I'd been wanting to contact. I hadn't been aware that he would be present, but I had been praying about trying to meet with him about a specific need in our ministry. When he walked into the room and we started talking, Ron nudged me from behind. Later he told me that perhaps we had been invited to that meeting because God was tired of my waiting to figure out how to make contact with this individual. Maybe God wanted us in that room so he could answer our prayer.

Ron was right. It hadn't been part of my plan to attend such a meeting, but God did have a plan. We were facing a swollen Jordan River in our ministry, and we'd been praying about how to cross it . . . and God dropped the plan right into our laps, yet we might have missed it if we'd followed our own "best judgment."

Although Jordan River crossings are not something most of us would choose, they are crucial in our lives. They develop our leadership skills. They define us, helping us become the people God wants us to be. Let me explain three ways in which those Jordan River obstacles in your life are actually a gift from God.

Jordan River crossings teach us that God's ways are better than our own. The method God used to get Joshua and the people across the flooded river—miraculously holding back the river's flow, allowing the people to cross on dry ground—was not something even the most experienced or creative leader could have fathomed. It wasn't remotely possible, in the human realm; but with God all things are possible. Successfully crossing our difficulties in God's miraculous way helps us not to panic the next time we see no way out. God's ways are higher than ours. When we follow him, we don't have to agonize while we wait to see what he has planned.

God uses our Jordan River crossings to increase our stature

and validate our leadership. God told Joshua, "Today I will begin to make you a great leader in the eyes of all the Israelites. They will know that I am with you, just as I was with Moses" (Joshua 3:7). The challenges we overcome with God's help validate our leadership and make it easier to do the task to which God has called us because we have the support and acknowledgment of the people we lead.

Jordan River crossings increase our faith and strength for the future. In Joshua 3:10–11, Joshua told the people of Israel, "Today you will know that the living God is among you. He will surely drive out the Canaanites, Hittites, Hivites, Perizzites, Girgashites, Amorites, and Jebusites ahead of you. Look, the Ark of the Covenant, which belongs to the Lord of the whole earth, will lead you across the Jordan River!" Joshua recognized that when God drove back the raging waters of the Jordan at flood stage, the people would understand that surely he could drive out the enemies that would confront them when they entered the Promised Land. The same is true for us today. When God delivers us or makes a way where there is no way, our faith in God's power and desire to help us grows. The next trial or impassible Jordan we face won't seem so big or scary.

We all must cross our own Jordans. Tragedy will surely come our way; it's unavoidable. But God's method of helping Joshua and the Israelites is also an encouragement to us. When we come to these difficult places in life, places that may seem too much to bear, God has promised to give us victory through him. The Lord your God is with you, just as he was with Moses and Joshua. He can make a way where there is no way.

SOMETIMES WE face rivers just ahead of us with no real plan for the crossing. We strategize, we stress out, we worry, but we still come up with no really good plan. Just how does one cross his or her Jordan? In modern terms, the Jordan River we face represents a challenge, a dilemma, a tragedy or a heartbreak that comes our way when we least expect it. These are things of life that catch us completely off guard and cause distress, much like that day in May when my dad went home to be with the Lord.

Crossing life's rivers is always a major challenge. While God does promise to be with us, it still requires us to take a step of faith . . . to step out in the midst of hurt and pain and into the great unknown. But to cross a river means that we have risen above the crisis we face and we are willing to forge ahead. A river can certainly be dangerous. Like the Jordan when Joshua approached, our river might be raging and overflowing its banks. We might be swept away by the current that is running strong. We might meet hazards along the way for which we aren't prepared. We might be tempted to turn back when the journey seems toughest. We might even drown.

Crossing a river alone is certainly more risky than crossing it with a friend, especially if that friend is the One who is undaunted by any river . . . if that friend is the One who created that river with a mere whisper. When we realize that we don't have to make it alone, we're freed to understand God's grace and God's provision in our lives. When the road seems darkest, he is the Light.

It's not so difficult to follow God's leading in unfamiliar circumstances when we recognize that he knows the way—and we don't. Joshua 3:3–4 records this instruction for the Israelites prior to their crossing the Jordan: "When you see the Levitical priests carrying the Ark of the Covenant of the LORD your God, move out from your positions and follow them. Since you have never traveled this way before, they will guide you."

We often come to rivers or paths that we have never before

crossed. A spouse dies. One of our parents dies. A trusted friend betrays us. A husband or wife abandons us, and we feel utterly alone. A child forsakes his or her relationship with Christ and starts down the road to destruction. We lose our job at a time when we need it most. We get a bad report from the doctor. When these situations occur, we need to see them as the beginning of a journey. It may be an undesired journey, but it is a journey upon which we must embark. We have no choice but to travel this road. Yet we must understand that the journey will be impossible if we depend on our own abilities to navigate the course. We must lean on God and God alone, for he alone knows the way we should take.

In Joshua 3 the people went down to the river and prepared to do exactly what God had commanded. Although they believed in God's plan, they didn't simply forge ahead. They knew God would deliver them, yet they waited. They waited three days. Why? Because they faced a challenge of immense proportion, and they knew they didn't have what it would take to cross the river on their own. They knew that only God could show them what to do next, only God could make a way. So they waited.

They listened for God's direction so they wouldn't be stepping out in their own wisdom or power. They prepared, but they waited. How many times I have faced this kind of situation in my own life. I've come to a river that I must cross, and unfortunately, many times I've forged ahead without waiting. I knew I had to cross, so I did. How much better it would have been simply to seek God and wait for his perfect plan for the crossing.

After Dad died, I began to understand how the children of Israel felt when they were waiting on God at the edge of that raging river. I sensed their trepidation as they waited on its banks. I felt the uneasiness that gave them pause. But from those feelings I started to see

God's hand moving and guiding me for the days ahead. During the grueling days following Dad's death, I discovered the wisdom and great reward that come from patiently waiting on God. I had no other choice. I was reeling inside and had no idea what course I should take. But I quickly learned that's where God wants us to be. At the end of our rope is where God shows up. This is where we find God's great power and comfort before the crossing.

God did not fail Joshua and the people. He had a plan. The priests were to lead the people up to those raging waters and walk straight into the river. And when the people took that courageous step, fully believing that God would not abandon them, he stacked up those rushing waters. The people didn't cross in mud puddles and muck. The Bible says that "the priests who were carrying the Ark of the LORD's Covenant stood on dry ground in the middle of the riverbed as the people passed by" (Joshua 3:17). What a miracle!

God doesn't mess around; he's got it all under control. Think of what he did in that place. Moments before, the waters raged; but now the ground was dry. Not muddy, not slippery, but dry. That's the deliverance God offers.

Do you believe that the same God who delivered Joshua and the people of Israel can still do great miracles today? When you face a raging river that seems impossible to cross, do you believe God will calm the waters? If only we would trust him every day, in every situation of our lives, for this type of miracle. If only we would trust him in the midst of our challenges. If only we would understand that God's ways are above our ways, that he works good from even the most desperate situations in our lives, that he receives glory when we trust him as we face our seemingly uncrossable rivers. When we embrace that truth and accept even dire circumstances with trust and peace, then we will be ready to live out this one great truth: "Not I, but Christ."

━━━━━━━━

AFTER THE children of Israel crossed this powerful river, with the water heaped up like mountains around them, God wanted them to remember what he had done. He told Joshua to call together the twelve leaders of the tribes of Israel and instruct each of them to carry away a stone from the river so that future generations could understand God's deliverance. Joshua told these leaders, "In the future your children will ask you, 'What do these stones mean?' Then you can tell them, 'They remind us that the Jordan River stopped flowing when the Ark of the LORD's Covenant went across.' These stones will stand as a memorial among the people of Israel forever" (Joshua 4:6–7).

Just as God had delivered them forty years earlier at the Red Sea, so now God had delivered them at the Jordan. He had performed a miracle in the midst of their great challenge, and he wanted that episode to be an encouragement to future generations so they could know his power and authority and goodness. Many times in life we rejoice when God delivers us from great challenges and struggles, only to forget about it in short order. We need to remember the work of God in our lives. We need to memorialize those miracle moments when God does his greatest work in the lives of believers.

I firmly believe that we today need to consider setting up our own "memorial stones" when we experience God's deliverance. First Samuel 7:7–12 recounts the story of God's miraculously delivering his children when the powerful Philistines attacked them. To mark the victory, Samuel set up a large stone as a rock of remembrance.

"He named it Ebenezer (which means 'the stone of help'), for he said, 'Up to this point the Lord has helped us!' " (1 Samuel 7:12). Every time the children of Israel looked at that rock, it reminded them that God had been faithful before and would be faithful again, no matter what danger or trial they might face. We, too, need to be reminded of God's grace in our lives. In our humanity, we tend to forget how good God has been to us. We must always remember how God takes us by the hand and leads us through violent rivers and dark paths of pain and doubt. Let us always remember our deliverer and all he has done for us.

To be sure, it's not practical for people today to collect boulders every time God does a miracle in their lives. We can't stack them up at the entrance to our homes so that we and everyone who ever enters that dwelling will know what God has done for us. All the same, we need to remember. Memorials in our lives help us remember the source of our deliverance when we face new challenges and struggles.

Maybe your memorial is something as simple as writing in a journal the story of God's provision in the midst of tribulation. Maybe it's talking about it with friends and family so they can rejoice with you in this great victory. Whatever it might be, remembering is important.

In our nation's capital many memorials have been built to honor great men and women. Several years ago Shari and I took our four children to Washington DC for a brief vacation to see the historical sights. We strolled along the National Mall, pointing out various divisions of the Smithsonian Institution. We visited the National Air and Space Museum, where the kids were enthralled by the airplanes and space vehicles on display. Later we climbed the great steps leading up to the Capitol. I took photos of the kids as they sat on the white marble railings that encompass that majestic building.

Then we came to the White House. Our children poked their heads through the black wrought-iron fence posts that surround this historic home. We took photos of them in front of the fence and moved on to the far end of the Mall.

We soon found ourselves walking by the reflecting pool that leads up to the Lincoln Memorial. I shared with the kids how hundreds of thousands of people had stood in that spot years earlier to hear Martin Luther King Jr. deliver his famous "I have a dream" speech. I explained the lasting impact that speech had made on our nation. We climbed the memorial's alabaster steps and arrived at the feet of the statue of Abraham Lincoln.

We stood there simply staring, reflecting on the life of this great American. I couldn't help but wonder what President Lincoln was like in person. How I would love to have a conversation with him, to hear some of his famous, down-to-earth wit from his own mouth rather than from a book. Our oldest son, Jonathan Jr., asked, "Dad, why did they build this big building just to put this statue inside of it?" I told him, "So that everyone who would ever come here would know what he did for our country."

That's precisely the reason we need memorials in our own lives— so that all who see them will know what God has done. And the greatest memorial we can build, really, is ourselves. People should be able to look at us and see the amazing power of God within us.

My dad read from the book *My Utmost for His Highest* by Oswald Chambers every day. He started each morning by reading the Bible, then a selection from Chambers's book. It's broken down into 365 daily readings, and Dad found within them inspiration for his daily life. Soon after Dad's death, I picked up his copy of that book and flipped through it. The following reading caught my attention:

> God is the Master Designer, and He allows adversities
> into your life to see if you can jump over them properly—
> "By my God I can leap over a wall" (Psalm 18:29). God
> will never shield you from the requirements of being His
> son or daughter. First Peter 4:12 says, "Beloved, do not
> think it strange concerning the fiery trial which is to try
> you, as though some strange thing happened to you. . . ."
> Rise to the occasion—do what the trial demands of you.
> It does not matter how much it hurts as long as it gives
> God the opportunity to manifest the life of Jesus in your
> body.

I read this passage several times and was struck by its words. It seemed to have a perfect correlation with Spurgeon's message that ended with the quote from Galatians: "Not I, but Christ." "Rise to the occasion—do what the trial demands of you. It does not matter how much it hurts as long as it gives God the opportunity to manifest the life of Jesus in your body." In other words, what God is doing in us will serve to show the world his power and his love. And it will also give us the opportunity to experience the victory in our lives that can only come from God's great strength.

I then noticed that those powerful words in Chambers's book, written early in the twentieth century, were in the reading for May 15. These were the words my dad had read just hours before his death. They were, quite likely, the last words he ever read on this earth. Again God was speaking to me through what seemed a chance collection of words . . . words made special because they were those my dad read on the day of his death—and because he lived them throughout his life.

The trials and challenges we face have a purpose: to give God the opportunity to manifest himself in us and miraculously deliver us and make us stronger. With God's help you can cross any river, overcome any obstacle. Rise to the occasion!

MAKE NO mistake; we all have raging rivers or trials to face. Sometimes the trial or challenge is not that great. Sometimes the examination is so great and our strength is so small, we feel overwhelmed. The trials and challenges we face have a purpose: to give God the opportunity to manifest himself in us and to give him the opportunity to miraculously deliver us and make us stronger. They are a test, but God has given us everything we need to meet the challenge. With God's help you can cross any river, overcome any obstacle. We can rise to the occasion if we allow God's promises to flow through us!

QUESTIONS TO CONSIDER

1. When you come to a powerful raging river overflowing its banks, do you look to yourself for solutions or do you look to God?
2. What test are you facing right now where you need to (with God's help) rise to the occasion?
3. Look back over this chapter. What is one promise that you could claim from God's Word to help you cross the raging river?

UPWARD LOOK:

Dear God, I recognize that you are what I need when I face the smooth-flowing streams of life and you are what I need when I face the raging rivers of testing. Thank you that you have promised to never leave or forsake me. Thank you that you have promised even to be close to me when I go through trials and testing. In Jesus' name, amen.

6

Not My Provision,
but God's

T HE PAST HAD been glorious—the stuff of stories—for Israel as well as for Thomas Road Baptist Church and Liberty University. Looking back, it's easy to see God's hand at work, his miraculous provision, and his special relationship with the people. But what about the future? Would that unique distinction, that divine blessing, persist even after the death of a pivotal founding figure?

Yes! In both cases, the resounding answer is *yes!* God uses people to do his work, but his work is not dependent on those people. In fact, just the opposite: those God uses are—and must be—dependent upon *him, his* call, *his* provision, and *his* encouragement.

From our vantage point today, it's natural to view the "children of Israel" as one monolithic people instead of as different individuals in different generations with different experiences. How could God's chosen people ever question God's calling, his provision for their needs, or their own special relationship with him after having experienced that supernatural deliverance from slavery in Egypt as well as God's miraculous provision of food and water in the desert? One simple answer is that most of the people who prepared to follow Joshua into the Promised Land hadn't been around for most of those "good old days." Many had not yet been born; others had been too young to remember or recognize the significance and the source of Israel's divine blessing. For about as many years as I had been alive before my dad's death—forty years—the Israelites had been in a holding pattern, camped in the wilderness just outside Canaan. It was the only life many of them had known.

Early on, God renewed his covenant with this second generation of Israelites by telling Joshua that all the men and boys should be circumcised. Circumcision had long been the symbol of God's special relationship and eternal covenant with the people of Israel. In giving Abraham the rite of circumcision many years earlier, God had said, "I will confirm my covenant with you and your descendants after you, from generation to generation. This is the everlasting covenant: I will always be your God and the God of your descendants after you. And I will give the entire land of Canaan, where you now live as a foreigner, to you and your descendants. It will be their possession forever, and I will be their God" (Genesis 17:7–8).

By having the Israelites circumcised, God was renewing that covenant, linking them to their great past, and drawing them into that special relationship with God that had marked their ancestors. What's more, they were the generation of promise. Many years earlier, God had been speaking of them. Their great ancestors Abraham,

Isaac, Jacob, and Moses had eagerly anticipated events that would be fulfilled in this generation's lifetime.

Their first celebration of the Passover in the land of Canaan reinforced that truth, linking them to the great history of their nation while anticipating the special part they, too, would play in the story. After all, years earlier, when God had instituted Passover, he had seen and spoken of this very time when they would celebrate it in the land he would give them. "Remember, these instructions are a permanent law that you and your descendants must observe forever. When you enter the land the LORD has promised to give you, you will continue to observe this ceremony" (Exodus 12:24–25). How reassuring to be accepted into and connected to a glorious past while knowing that your life and ministry are part of the blessings and fulfillment of God's promises to those who have gone before you.

God's gracious actions toward this second generation of liberated Israelites are encouraging to all of us who have come later: all second-generation, third-, fourth-, or subsequent-generation heirs to God's promises. Like me. Like today's Thomas Road Baptist Church. And probably like you. Second-generation people always must grapple with the issue of what parts of the past still apply to them, even as they struggle to discern their path into the future. How do we balance the two? Is it too presumptuous even to assume that we can be heirs to the promises God made to our forebears? Good news: the answer is no. God wants to use us, bless us, and provide for us as we carry the mantle of ministry into the future.

Following Dad's death, I came to believe that God wanted to call our church to a greater work. It would have been easy for us to simply coast on all that God had performed in the nearly fifty-one years of our church history. God had used Dad in amazing ways during that time. Millions of people had heard the gospel as a result. Tens of thousands had been educated through our school system. Many thousands more were attending our services. Untold numbers of other churches had been planted.

Or we could have wondered whether we could even presume to be part of the continuing story. We could have let that stop us from moving forward.

But God wanted more from us. He wanted us to reach out as we'd never done before, even though this might not have seemed logical so soon after a time of loss. God wants to assure us that his promises and provision are for us in this generation, at this time, just as they were in the time of our ancestors. He wants to give us a brand-new vision that, while connected to the past, will carry us into the future.

Many times in the last year of Dad's life, he proclaimed that he was trusting God to do more in the next five years of our ministry than in the previous fifty years. That's a clear example of the new vision God gives to us as we march forward in his great power.

So now the question is, how can we accomplish all that God has planned for us? Like those who preceded us, we cannot do it in our own strength. We must depend on God to provide the resources and encouragement we'll need to win each new victory as we move forward with him. After all, he is Jehovah-Jireh, the God who provides.

God's Provision

JUST AFTER the people celebrated that first Passover in the Promised Land, we read of a major shift that affected the daily lives of God's people forevermore: "While the Israelites were camped at Gilgal on the plains of Jericho, they celebrated Passover on the evening of the fourteenth day of the first month. The very next day they began to eat unleavened bread and roasted grain harvested from the land. No manna appeared on the day they first ate from the crops of the land, and it was never seen again. So from that time on the Israelites ate from the crops of Canaan" (Joshua 5:10–12).

Why are these verses so significant? Because God now had a new provision for his children. You see, for forty years in the wilderness, these people had been eating manna, which literally means, "What is it?" They didn't even really understand what they were eating. Forty years earlier, the people of Israel had cried out in frustration to Moses because they didn't have food. They complained that, even though they had been slaves in Egypt, Moses had led them away from the safety of that land into the wilderness with no provisions. They claimed that Moses had led them there to die.

Moses cried out to God for wisdom—and for food. And God answered both requests. Not only did he show Moses how he would provide for the children of Israel; he also sent a hitherto-unknown substance that would sustain them and would miraculously arrive fresh for them each day. This substance became known as manna. It was strange to the people, but they quickly learned that it would suffice in their time of need. God had again provided for them during a time of crisis.

For forty years God had been sustaining his children with this heavenly food. Now he had a new provision for his people. Instead of focusing on the opportunity, the children of Israel could have focused on the loss. Why did God's provision suddenly stop? What would they do without the manna they'd depended on for so long? But focusing on the loss would have been foolish. God had something far better in store for his people.

The children of Israel would no longer need to be consumed

with mere survival; now God would give them more than enough to survive, thrive, and succeed. They went from existing on manna to feasting on all the bountiful foods of Canaan. They went from wandering in the wilderness to taking possession of the Promised Land. This was a fundamental shift in their mind-set and circumstance, and it was the continuation of the fulfillment of God's promises to Abraham many years earlier.

After we go through spiritual or physical or emotional battles in our lives, isn't it comforting to know that God has a new provision in store for us, just as he did for the nation of Israel? This gives us great hope that even when we're in the midst of spiritual doldrums, a better day is coming. The children of Israel had eaten the same food every day for breakfast, lunch, and dinner—for forty years. Talk about doldrums! Now they were ready for change.

My wife often complains about my food habits. Virtually every day of my life, for as long as I can remember, I have eaten Pop-Tarts for breakfast. I love them. I rarely eat anything else in the morning. I also could easily go to the same restaurant for lunch and dinner every day. It wouldn't bother me at all. Many days, after my usual Pop-Tarts breakfast, I've gone to McDonald's for both lunch and dinner. Shari can't understand this. She'd like to go to a different restaurant for every meal, or at least try a different recipe or dish for every meal if we're eating at home. She doesn't comprehend how anyone could be satisfied eating the exact same thing for breakfast, lunch, and dinner virtually every day of his life. Yet that is exactly what the Israelites had been doing for forty years.

Now, understand, there was nothing wrong with God's manna. It had been nothing short of miraculous, and all the people of Israel knew it was a gift directly from God. But God still had more amazing provisions in store.

The miraculous provision of manna had run its course, and God wanted to do even more amazing things for his people. In our own lives, after a time, God's provisions may become commonplace, expected, or even "stale." We may hunger for something fresh but fear losing the comfort and security of God's current provision. But we don't have to worry. God can provide for us today and in the future just as surely as he has in the past. "Taste and see that the LORD is good. Oh, the joys of those who take refuge in him!" (Psalm 34:8). God is prepared to offer you new provisions. He has miracles ahead that will do nothing less than amaze you at his great care and love for his children.

God's Encouragement

SOMETIMES WHAT we need from God is not physical but spiritual and emotional. God knows what it means to be human—he created us. He knows that we often need divine encouragement to strengthen us for the tasks to which we're called. And God graciously provides the encouragement we need to go on. Read the words of Joshua 5:13–15:

> When Joshua was near the town of Jericho, he looked up and saw a man standing in front of him with sword in hand. Joshua went up to him and demanded, "Are you friend or foe?"
>
> "Neither one," he replied. "I am the commander of the LORD's army."
>
> At this, Joshua fell with his face to the ground in reverence. "I am at your command," Joshua said. "What do you want your servant to do?"

The commander of the LORD's army replied, "Take off your sandals, for the place where you are standing is holy." And Joshua did as he was told.

Joshua had lifted his eyes and was looking toward Jericho, the next great challenge he and the people would face. Jericho, the oldest inhabited city in the world, was not like other cities. This great city had not one but two walls surrounding it, a sign to the world that it would not be easily conquered. The outer wall was constructed of stone, the inner wall of brick. Both seemed impenetrable. Could a practically untested band of nomads be victorious against Jericho? It would be another major challenge for the children of Israel.

As Joshua contemplated the daunting task before him, he looked up and saw a man with a sword. Joshua had a typical human response to this armed figure: "Are you friend or foe?" (Joshua 5:13). But this was no ordinary man. It was the Lord himself, and he had a message of hope and encouragement for Joshua.

Joshua was looking upon the very face of God. This is what theologians call a theophany—a temporary vision of God given to his people for the purpose of encouragement. Every time a theophany occurred in the Old Testament, God was about to move his children in a new way. In each case he called them beyond the confines of their limited faith and out of their comfort zones.

Joshua must have been wondering, *What am I going to do now?* He knew he was up against a people who were strong and well protected. Even after the miraculous crossing of the Jordan River, how could he help but see the seemingly insurmountable obstacles threatening to prevent him from conquering the well-fortified city of Jericho? But God, in all of his wisdom, decided that Joshua needed a pep talk.

God does not leave us alone to face our battles with no direction. He doesn't simply lead us across our Jordans to drop us on the other side with no vision for moving forward. He wants to give us the encouragement we need to carry on and win the victory. He wants to show us why we had to go through those trials and how they will prepare us for the future.

God appeared to Joshua to give him the encouragement and direction he would need for the future. He told Joshua that he would deliver Jericho into his hands in spite of the intimidating walls. He wants to do the same for us. And while we may not be facing literal walls of stone and brick, we do face symbolic walls in our lives. Yet God can give us victory over every one of them. He stands ready to use us and to take us to new heights.

Can you imagine how Joshua must have felt standing in the presence of almighty God? He'd surely heard Moses often tell how he'd stood in God's presence at the burning bush, and now here he was in a similar situation. His heart must have been pounding, and his legs probably threatened to betray him. He was standing with God!

I imagine it was then that he knew he could carry on, that he could lead the people forward to do God's will. Standing with God empowered him to carry out the new vision he'd been given. His strength came not from his own power or abilities but because he had been reminded of God's presence. He had been reminded that God was there with them, every step of the way.

Today we don't look for God to show up in the middle of the road, talking to us as he did with Moses and Joshua. We're never going to see a burning bush or an angelic, glorified Man standing before us. But we will have fresh encounters with God. In fact, the kind of encounter he is calling us to can actually be far more personal, far more powerful, far more meaningful than even what

Moses and Joshua had. This fresh encounter can be experienced each and every day through a powerful and personal prayer life. That is a conversation God wants to have with us on a regular basis. In 1 Thessalonians 5:16–18 the Bible tells us, "Always be joyful. Never stop praying. Be thankful in all circumstances, for this is God's will for you who belong to Christ Jesus." Prayer is part of God's will for us in everyday life. He wants to have a constant line of communication into our lives, just as he had with Moses and Joshua.

God is calling us to a fresh encounter that can continue through the rest of our lives. He had a great plan for Joshua. He knew that Jericho would be conquered. He simply required Joshua to follow his direction. Joshua had encountered God, had experienced his power, had felt his encouragement and sensed his presence. And as a result, he was ready for the task ahead.

We can be sure that God has a plan for us. He knows what lies ahead, and he knows the victories that are available to us when we make ourselves available to him. He knows what we will be able to accomplish in his power and in his presence. But when we miss out on fresh encounters with God, we miss out on what he has planned for us. We can't get the full measure of God's blessing this way. If Joshua had led the children of Israel across the Jordan River and then felt that God had been wrong, or if he had stopped listening to God and decided to battle Jericho in his own strength, the great miracle of victory over Jericho might never have occurred. Or God would have used someone else to accomplish his plan. I don't want to see my fresh encounter wasted because I give up halfway through God's plan. My dad often told audiences, "Don't quit." I believe that's a message God wants us to take to heart.

And that brings us to an important point. Just how do we know when God is ready to set his plan in motion in our lives? We won't likely have the same face-to-face meeting with God that Joshua did, but we still must prepare our hearts to be in God's presence. We prepare ourselves through prayer, as we've already discussed, and by pursuing holiness.

Leviticus 11:44–45 says, "I am the LORD your God. You must consecrate yourselves and be holy, because I am holy. . . . I, the LORD, am the one who brought you up from the land of Egypt, that I might be your God. Therefore, you must be holy because I am holy." Paul wrote, "Imitate me, just as I imitate Christ" (1 Corinthians 11:1). This is the pursuit of personal holiness.

When we prepare our hearts to receive God's plan, he will not leave us hanging. We may need to wait patiently for a season, but God will answer our prayers. Crossing our Jordan is a major step in the right direction. Once we've crossed the raging waters of whatever trial life places in our path, we must then prepare ourselves, through prayer and holiness, for our fresh encounter with God.

My father said in 1971, at the founding of Liberty University: "The only limit to what God can do in the life of the believer is how far that believer is willing to follow him. God never hesitates. He is just waiting for a people who are ready." I treasure those words. They are fixed in my heart, and I continually pray that I can live out my life in audacious faith the way Dad did.

How far are you willing to follow God? Are you ready to trust him? Are you ready to step up without hesitation and experience his mighty works in your own life? When you are, he'll provide what you need to get the job done.

REMEMBER, YOU must be willing to step out in faith. Faith is not only the capacity to see the invisible . . . it is the capacity to believe and to work to make it a reality. When God calls us to step out of the boat and to walk on water, we can do the impossible for God as long as we remember the source of all possibilities is God himself.

QUESTIONS TO CONSIDER

1. Remember a time when God met a great need in your life. How did you feel when you realized that it was God who met your need?
2. God gave the Israelites manna to eat for forty years; what are some things that God has faithfully provided in your life?
3. Following God requires audacious faith. What is something in your life that requires audacious faith?

UPWARD LOOK:

Dear God, thank you for your provision and your encouragement. I know I need you not only in the good times, but I especially need you when times are tough. Help me to lean on you every day, so that when the challenges come, I will naturally and easily turn to you for my provision and encouragement. In Jesus' name, amen.

7

Not My Strength, but God's

ON JULY 17, 1999, many Americans—and people around the world—were shocked when they woke to the news that John F. Kennedy Jr. was missing. He, his wife, Carolyn, and her sister, Lauren Bessette, had taken off from the Essex County Airport in Caldwell, New Jersey, on the previous evening. Kennedy planned to pilot the small plane to Martha's Vineyard and then on to Hyannis Port.

As they flew beyond the glow of city lights, they found themselves over water on what was becoming a dark, hazy night. The black Atlantic below them seemed to merge with the black sky above, and before long Kennedy couldn't tell the difference between the two. Not yet an instrument-rated pilot, he flew on into the dark expanse under visual flight rules. According to National Transportation Safety Board speculation, Kennedy became disoriented, and his plane spun out of control. All three lives were lost.

Their bodies and the plane's wreckage were not found until days later. In the ensuing investigation, it was determined that the plane's autopilot had not been engaged. Kennedy was flying the plane by hand. Had he used the autopilot, the three presumably would have made it safely to their destination.

So many times we try to go through life using only "visual flight rules"—relying on our own eyes and our own power—when God is right there, just like a plane's autopilot, ready to help us navigate the darkness ahead if we'll only let him. Relying on God's guidance when the way seems dark and hazy doesn't make those conditions go away, but it does ensure that we can travel safely through the darkness to our destination. A Christian's life is not free from dark times, discouragement, or despair; but no matter how disorienting the blackness we find ourselves flying in, we can trust God to be right there with us. When we need strength to continue, it is not our strength, but God's, that will see us through. When we feel lost in the darkness of despair, it is not our ability, but God's, that will bring the light of hope.

A Christian, like anyone, can get discouraged for many reasons. When we take our eyes off of God, we sometimes find ourselves stuck in a pothole on the road of life, completely knocked off the road, or even tumbling perilously over a cliff. During these times fear, worry, or discouragement can creep into our hearts. Other times it's the sheer monotony of our daily walk—feeling like we're not making progress, wondering when or if the end will ever come—that can weaken our resolve and make us susceptible to discouragement.

People can endure almost anything if it's brief. That's why we rip off a bandage or pluck a stray hair quickly. But the longer unpleasantness lingers—chronic pain, desperate loneliness after the death of a loved one, uncertainty about the future, not knowing where a prodigal child might be, waiting for the pink slip from your boss at a slowly failing business—the stress wears on us until we feel we can't possibly bear it any longer.

One week might seem like a mere bandage-yank compared with the length of time you've been waiting for a problem to resolve or a difficult situation to improve. But a week probably seemed like a long time indeed to Joshua and the army of Israel as they marched around the walls of Jericho each day. How could such actions possibly bring down the wall, they might have questioned. The plan was highly unusual and seemed ineffectual, from the human perspective. But God had commanded it, so they marched.

Some undoubtedly felt fear at being so close to a dangerous enemy who might attack from the wall at any moment. Others likely were frustrated at not being able to take action but being confined to walking passively around the enemy's stronghold without so much as a peep. Have either of these feelings discouraged you lately? The "battle" of Jericho gives us valuable insights into how to conquer discouragement when it seems we're stuck in an unpleasant holding pattern:

Rest in Your Purpose (Joshua 6:2–5)

JOSHUA AND the people marched at God's command, so they didn't have to second-guess the wisdom of their actions. Even when you don't see any progress or purpose in what you're doing, if you know it's what God told you to do, keep doing it.

Remain in God's Presence (Joshua 6:8)

THE ISRAELITES marched in the presence of the Lord. So must we. God's presence in our lives brings peace and joy in spite of the conditions around us.

Practice Obedience (Joshua 6:9–10)

GOD GAVE the Israelites specific instructions on how they were to march, when, with whom, and where. Perhaps the hardest part was the order to remain silent—no talking whatsoever. You probably know how hard it is not to complain or ask why when you've endured a time of darkness, discouragement, or God's apparent silence. What would have happened had one or more of the people disobeyed God's instructions? We don't know, because the people obeyed God in every point. So can we.

Patiently Persist (Joshua 6:11–16)

DOES IT feel as if you've been marching in the dark, alone, with little to show for it for a long time? Are you discouraged? Don't give up. You may just be starting the seventh day of your march, and if you just keep going a little longer, you'll see those stubborn walls of difficulty in your life fall down. Don't give in to discouragement and frustration. Press on in God's strength, not yours.

FEELING DOWN is part of being human. I've been there myself a few times. We should not be embarrassed to admit that we sometimes get disheartened in our Christian walk. Even pastors and great Christian leaders face despair. Even my father, who was the most upbeat and positive believer I've ever known, weathered a few periods of discouragement.

Becoming discouraged is normal. But as believers, we must be ever mindful that we have a great God living within us who is capable of carrying us through the dark valleys of life. I know how your heart can sink in the face of a daunting mountain blocking your progress or a seemingly unending night of despair. But you must not let discouragement tear you down or stop you in your tracks. Don't let tribulations take the joy out of your journey. God can and will bring you through life's challenges. He will also give you perspective that will encourage you in your most difficult times. I'm speaking from experience.

I've learned a lot about myself and my need to depend on God during the months since Dad's death. Some of the most important lessons God has taught me have been the following seven reminders that bring me daily comfort. I rehearse them often, and God encourages me through them. I pray they will encourage you, as well, as you confront life's problems with your hand placed firmly within the powerful grasp of our wonderful Lord.

The End Is Worth the Beginning

I OFTEN liken life to the building of a house. At the point where the framing is complete, the roof is going on, and the project is finally beginning to resemble a house, the owners start to see their dreams taking shape, and they get more excited about the prospect of their home being finished. But at this point the owners also may become disheartened that moving in still seems a long way off. A lot of work remains to be done. Unforeseen problems, additional costs, and delays the owners did not anticipate come into play. They begin to realize that there are going to be ups and downs and a few bumps and bruises before they can even think about moving into their new home.

I'm sure a lot of families in this situation have grown discouraged by the long process and wondered if they'd ever have the house they dreamed of at the beginning or if it'll be worth all the time, expense, and hassle. That's where faith is required: the end is worth the beginning. Wait for it.

We may see a similar pattern in our lives. Things seem to be going just fine as we build our lives and our dreams: the foundation, frame, and roof of our lives are strong, and we're growing stronger spiritually. But suddenly problems beset us. Satan tries to move in. He wants to convince us that our "house" will never be complete and that we'll never be a finished project. If we listen to him instead of keeping our eyes on the finished product of our faith, we'll get bogged down in our present problems and the building projects of our lives will get terribly sidetracked.

Philippians 1:6 was one of my father's favorite verses. I never asked him why he loved it so much, but I have to believe it was because he was able to endure many of his life's challenges by resting on its promise: "God, who began the good work within you, will continue his work until it is finally finished on the day when Christ Jesus returns." When discouragement besets you, claim this promise. God has begun a good work in you, and he wants to finish it. What an honor it is to have God actively involved in our lives!

We must remain focused on the end, not the present. We must concentrate on what will come instead of what has bogged us down. And we must continue to be motivated by the vision that Christ has set within us and remain true to what we will one day be through him. What better way to defeat discouragement!

The Reward Is Worth the Cost

WHEN OUR Christian walk starts to cost us something we value— the respect of friends or the world, our livelihood, time we don't feel we have, effort we feel too weak to give—we may wonder if it's worth it and thus begin the descent into discouragement. We forget that God is our foundation and strength. Most pastors can recount examples of people who once diligently worked for Christ . . . until the cost of faithfully following him and obeying his commandments knocked them off track. Sometimes these people return to their faith later, but too often they remain locked in disillusionment with life and God. What a tragedy it is when we refuse to allow God to help us through our trials.

I imagine most of us can recall a time when we reached "rock bottom." I don't think anyone is exempt from the deep emotional pain or spiritual anguish of wondering if working for God is worth what it costs us. When I am confronted with these emotions, I often remember the words of Paul, encouraging us to remember that what we gain in Christ is worth any cost: "Whatever was to my profit I now consider loss for the sake of Christ. What is more, I consider everything a loss compared to the surpassing greatness of knowing Christ Jesus my Lord, for whose sake I have lost all things. I consider them rubbish, that I may gain Christ" (Philippians 3:7–8 NIV). Our life in Christ is always worth the cost of following him.

The Challenge Is Worth the Effort

AT THE beginning of a long road trip, have you ever despaired when realizing the many hours of driving still ahead of you? Life is sometimes like that too. In the aftermath of an especially rough trial or tribulation, some Christians are similarly taken aback by the long road of recovery that lies before them. They say, "I can't make it. It's too great a challenge for me." They give up—not on themselves, but on God. We must never allow ourselves to get to this point. We must persevere and move forward with the Spirit of God working within us. Why? Because the reward is always great when we are doing God's work, especially when we are trusting him to bring us out of a profound personal or family crisis. The apostle Paul understood the importance of continued effort to rise to the challenge: "I press on to reach the end of the race and receive the heavenly prize for which God, through Christ Jesus, is calling us" (Philippians 3:14).

Paul's example encourages us to do just what he did: carry on the fight, persevere with passion, and face the challenge with the goal of glorifying God in mind. I must say that the reality of God's upward calling became much more real to me during my own trek through a spiritual abyss following my father's death. As a result of allowing God to carry me through that terrible crisis, I am now more committed than ever to facing the challenges of life because I have seen the hand of God actively and wondrously at work within me. I know the challenge is worth any effort.

The Vision Is Worth the Pain

No matter how overwhelming and seemingly intolerable the pain and difficulty you may be facing, it pales in comparison with God's glory that shall be revealed in us through that suffering. As 2 Corinthians 4:17–18 says, "Our present troubles are small and won't last very long. Yet they produce for us a glory that vastly outweighs them and will last forever! So we don't look at the troubles we can see now [our pain]; rather, we fix our gaze on things that cannot be seen [God's glory]. For the things we see now will soon be gone, but the things we cannot see will last forever."

Look beyond your troubles with eyes of faith. The vision of God's glory yet to come makes even the traumatic losses and trials of this present life worth it all—and a bit easier to bear. Why does an athlete arduously, painfully beat his or her body into shape? For the opportunity to win the race. Why does a person put up with eating "rabbit food" and say no to rich, fattening desserts? Because it's worth it to him or her to look better, feel younger, and salvage his or her health. Why would anyone elect to go through the pain of cosmetic surgery or hip replacement? Because the pain is temporary while the gain is long-term. Why does a woman endure morning sickness, a ballooning body, and the pain of childbirth? Because the vision of the child to come is worth the pain.

When we fix our eyes on the vision of God's glory and what he will accomplish in us through our suffering, the pain is no longer our focus. Our outlook improves as we see the bigger picture and recognize that the vision is always worth the pain. And even if we can't see the end result or how God will be glorified through our suffering, we can have confidence in his goodness and ability to work things for our good and his glory. Even when we can't see it clearly from the midst of our hurt, what is to come in God is always worth the pain.

No matter what your pain, take your eyes off what you're suffering and turn them on Jesus. Ask him to be glorified in the midst of your struggle. Ask him to help you have faith to see a vision of his glory. The good news is that whatever you're enduring, the trial and your suffering are temporary, and God will receive glory when you live out "Not I, but Christ" in your ordeal. As 2 Corinthians 4:16 says, "That is why we never give up. Though our bodies are dying, our spirits are being renewed every day."

The Victory Is Worth the Wait

I F   Y O U   could have asked anyone in the army of Israel after the fall of Jericho, he would have told you in no uncertain terms: "The victory was worth the wait!" Few victories come quickly. More often than not, we have to wait . . . and endure sorrow, uncertainty, discomfort, and fatigue. But God gives victory to those who wait for him to move. In his perfect time, God delivers us, and the struggle of waiting is replaced by the sweet joy of victory.

In these last several months of leading Thomas Road Baptist Church, I've found that the emotional distress I experienced has slowly faded as God allows me the privilege of witnessing many victories in my life and in the lives of others. Every time someone comes to our church and accepts Christ as Savior, that's a victory. Every time one of our members kneels at the altar and pleads with God for the salvation of a loved one, friend, or neighbor, that's a victory. Every time someone rises out of the waters of our baptistery, that's a victory. These occurrences provide spiritual fuel to me as a pastor. In my personal life, every time I see my children talking about the blessings of God, that's a victory. Every time my wife shares with me a spiritual truth she has learned, that's a victory.

When we stop to think, it becomes apparent that God blesses our lives with many victories. We need to acknowledge them. They are there to encourage us and to strengthen us in our walk of faith.

The Bible promises that God blesses those who wait upon him: "The LORD is good to those who wait for Him, to the soul who seeks Him" (Lamentations 3:25 NKJV). No matter what circumstance is troubling your heart or tearing at your mind, there is literally no situation in which it is too hard for the Lord to bring victory if you'll only wait for him. Waiting isn't easy, but God gives us the strength to carry on until he carries us to victory.

God Is Always at Work in Your Life

WHAT ARE your goals in life? What do you feel God has called you to accomplish? What do you know God has gifted you to do? Have you done as much or gotten as far as you'd hoped? It's okay if you haven't arrived yet; God's still working in your life. Why should we hope to be better than the apostle Paul, who described his life this way: "I don't mean to say that I have already achieved these things or that I have already reached perfection. But I press on to possess that perfection for which Christ Jesus first possessed me" (Philippians 3:12)? God is still working on you—it's his strength, not yours, that matters.

Don't get discouraged during those times when you realize you're not as strong or spiritually mature as some other Christians you may know. You're growing and will continue to grow. Perhaps those Christians who seem to have it so much more together than you do have been placed in your life to facilitate your Christian growth!

I'm afraid sometimes people think salvation is a miracle pill that's supposed to suddenly make all of our problems go away. Salvation is a gift, but it is not a magic potion that cures all ills. When God saves us, we embark on a journey of faith. And journeys take time. We will have days when we feel spiritually on top of the world, and we will have other days when we barely feel saved at all. In the lives of all Christians, there comes a point when we suddenly realize we're not spiritual supermen or superwomen.

God's advice is simple: continue to grow and allow him to work in your life. The apostle Peter gave wise instruction, encouraging believers to grow in grace just as a newborn baby experiences gradual growth each day: "Like newborn babies, you must crave pure spiritual milk so that you will grow into a full experience of salvation. Cry out for this nourishment, now that you have had a taste of the Lord's kindness" (1 Peter 2:2–3).

I have personally appreciated this encouragement in God's Word, especially when I suddenly found myself filling the pastoral position long held by my father, pastor, and spiritual mentor. I had to learn, though, that it was okay not to have it all together or know it all right up front. It's natural, expected, and even good to have to grow into the shoes God calls us to fill. We must never compare our lives to the lives of others, because God is doing a unique and individual work in each one of us. I take comfort in knowing that God wants me to be me—not Jerry Falwell—and that he wants to nourish me in unique ways. He has called me to accomplish his will for my life at a pace he has designed just for me.

Sometimes a Pause Is Needed to Experience God's Power

WHAT IF you spent almost all of your time at work and invested very little time in your family? You might have a productive work life, but your home life would almost certainly fall apart. We need to figure out how to balance the requirements of work so that we are also investing in our spouses and our children. The Christian life is similar. We cannot focus all our attention on ministry and outreach without taking regular time for personal growth through prayer and Bible study. Without routine time for spiritual nourishment and renewal, our ministry efforts will be empty and unsatisfying.

In chapter 18 of the Gospel of John, we see how even Jesus withdrew to a solitary place on the night before he was crucified so he could gain the unique power that comes through prayer. I want to focus on a subtle clue about Jesus' character in this passage, as John points it out: "Jesus crossed the Kidron Valley with his disciples and entered a grove of olive trees. Judas, the betrayer, knew this place, because Jesus had often gone there with his disciples" (verses 1–2). Notice that Jesus frequently escaped to this garden so he could pray. It was a routine of Jesus' prayer life. If even Jesus needed this type of prayerful getaway in his life, I know I certainly need it in mine. We all would do well to follow his pattern.

Jesus obviously felt it was important to escape from the routine of life—and he was certainly busy—so that he could pray. He took the disciples with him, showing them the need for balance in their own lives. Their ministry was important, but their need for spiritual renewal through prayer and close fellowship with the Father was just as essential. These prayer times were not considered "downtime." Rather, they were purposeful and necessary times of experiencing the power and essential nature of prayer for followers of Jesus. All believers, even pastors, must take this message to heart.

If we are commanded, according to 1 Corinthians 15:58, to steadfastly labor for the Lord, we must regularly pause for prayer, or we will not be able to maintain that intense level of activity or ministry. If we hope to be valuable laborers in the army of God, it's absolutely crucial that we include time for prayer each day. If we do not, we will fall into the trap of trying to accomplish things in our own strength. This is a prescription for failure. We must always remember this one great truth: "Not I, but Christ."

In my own life I've committed to balancing my many activities with patient and passionate prayer. I have encouraged our church congregation to also make regular time for prayer. We should be motivated not only by the fact that God is always at work in our lives but also by the fact that the more we are called to do, the greater our need for regular time away with God.

I encourage you to remember, during your busy day and life, that God craves time with you. He wants to hear your prayers and receive your praise and thanksgiving. The Christian life is so much more rewarding when we are spending time with God and focusing on his direction for our lives.

———————

ARE YOU discouraged? Are you wondering when God is going to bless you? Are you asking when God is going to meet your needs? Are you in a relationship that is falling apart? Are you a parent who is reeling in pain over a son or daughter who has wandered away from God? Are you lonely and feeling that no one cares for you?

Don't give up. Stand on these words: "Not I, but Christ." Not my strength, but his. Listen to God's encouragement:

Have you never heard? Have you never understood? The LORD is the everlasting God, the Creator of all the earth. He never grows weak or weary. No one can measure the depths of his understanding. He gives power to the weak and strength to the powerless. Even youths will become weak and tired, and young men will fall in exhaustion. But those who trust in the LORD will find new strength. They will soar high on wings like eagles. They will run and not grow weary. They will walk and not faint. (Isaiah 40:28–31)

Put your trust in the Lord today. Know that God is not done with you, no matter how dark your path may seem. You are his work in progress, and you can experience victory like you've never known if you will cast your cares on him. Experience freedom like you've never imagined and joy like you've never dreamed of by stepping out of your despair and into the strong arms of a loving God.

HAVE YOU ever attempted to lift something so heavy that you could not even budge it? No matter how hard you pulled or strained or groaned . . . the object would not move! That is very frustrating, isn't it? But have you ever noticed that if you got someone to help you lift the heavy load, it seemed as if it was a very light load? Your friend's help did not just lighten the load, but he or she gave you hope and courage to try yet again. Jesus says, "Come to me, all who are weary and heavy-laden, and I will give you rest" (Matthew 11:28 NASB). When we face heavy burdens, we need more strength, and more strength is available to the believer.

In this chapter we are encouraged to remember that God's strength and power are limitless. When we encounter heavy loads, we need to call out to the Lord in our weakness, and in our weakness his strength will be realized. There are many challenges that we will face, or have faced, where we must recognize that we are either in trouble, just out of trouble, or just about to get into trouble. Life is challenging, but with God's help we can not only face the challenges, but overcome the challenges.

QUESTIONS TO CONSIDER:

1. Can you remember a time when you were completely exhausted physically?
2. What about a time when you were exhausted emotionally?
3. What about a time when you were exhausted spiritually?
4. How did you renew your strength in each of the above areas?

UPWARD LOOK:

Dear God, thank you that when I run out of strength, you never run out of strength and encouragement. Thank you for the privilege of leaning on your strong arms in times of trial. Help me to trust in you every moment of every day. In Jesus' name, amen.

8

Not My Priorities, but God's

NOT LONG AFTER Dad passed away and I became the pastor of Thomas Road Baptist Church, I realized that my schedule would never be the same. I became almost overwhelmed with the sudden influx of meetings, phone calls, church visitations, and many other responsibilities that go with the territory of being a pastor. I was committed to meeting the needs of those in my congregation as well as many others. Further, Dad had been scheduled to attend numerous events, and I wanted to honor those commitments by appearing in his stead. Soon I found my calendar full of events that were taking me away more and more from my family and church responsibilities.

One night I was working in my bedroom office on my laptop while the children were climbing all over the bed and playing with our dog. They were having a great time and, as you might imagine, they were getting a bit boisterous. Unable to focus on my work, I asked my son Nicholas if he could take the other kids somewhere else to play. He looked back at me and said he didn't want to because he wanted to spend time with me. Then he added, "I wish Poppy [my dad] was still alive so I could see you more." Those words cut into my heart that night. In his innocence, my son had shown me that I was allowing seemingly important things to take the place of the truly important things in my life—namely, my family.

Too often we allow the trivial things in our lives to take precedence over the things that have eternal significance. When this happens, you can be sure it will keep you from experiencing all that God wants to do in your life. God wants you to experience life in spectacular ways. He wants you to breathe in the intoxicating air of his presence, and we must determine to allow nothing to ever hinder that experience. But we need his help.

Let's take a biblical look at this concept. In 2 Chronicles 5 we read of Solomon's care while inaugurating the newly built temple in Jerusalem. It was the most spectacular temple in the ancient world. The courtyard provided ample space for the people of God to enter his presence to worship. The building itself housed both the Holy Place, where the priests ministered, and the Holy of Holies, where the glory of God resided on the Ark of the Covenant. It was truly God's house, and it became the centerpiece of Israel's national, corporate, and spiritual life.

When the time came to dedicate the temple, the priests and musicians sang and ministered to those who had gathered there. But almost immediately a great cloud descended on the temple. The cloud became so thick that the priests and musicians had to stop doing what they were supposed to be doing because they couldn't see. That cloud represented the amazing presence of God in that place. And when his presence became that real and significant, the priests and musicians had to stop trying to do anything other than focus on him.

This is a picture of God's relationship with his people in the Old Testament, but it also provides a spiritual picture of what we can experience in our own lives. Many times we get so busy that we miss our own cloud, our own visit from God. If we're not careful, our focus will be on what we're doing for God instead of who he is and what he is doing for us.

A friend of mine, many years ago, felt that God was calling him to become a preacher. He was passionate about serving God and wanted to preach in churches everywhere because he had been given a great gift in terms of ability to communicate powerfully. He began speaking in churches and seeing amazing results. That's when he started to get impressed with his own abilities. He started to believe his own hype, and tragically, he forgot the Giver of those abilities. My friend started focusing less on God's power in his life and more on his own abilities. It wasn't long before he found himself in a great deal of trouble because of some decisions he had made in his personal life.

Why did this happen? This man was a gifted communicator and was being used in a powerful way to help many people. The reason is this: he began focusing on the outward expression of God's power instead of the inward experience of that power. That's a prescription for failure. You see, in order to find God's true power and blessing in our lives, we must stand back, like those priests and musicians in the temple, and let the cloud of God's presence envelop our lives. We may be able to do things for God, but it is far more important that we simply be in God's presence, letting him do what he desires through us. This is the prescription for happiness and contentment. It's the real secret to living the one great truth found in Galatians 2:20, "Not I, but Christ." These words are the New Testament expression of the Old Testament cloud of God's magnificent presence, and just as that cloud directed the Israelites, so Christ can direct our lives today. He wants to permeate all that we do and be wholly present in our lives to the point that we have to stop and, in awe, experience his majesty just as the priests and musicians did in the temple long ago. The power of Jesus Christ is just as real today as it was then. He can descend upon our hearts and give us everything we need in order to do what he calls us to do.

In our modern society, we are inundated with distractions that keep us from experiencing that wondrous cloud of God's presence in our lives. Time is often our worst enemy when it comes to living out our faith. There is a constant taxing of our time in every area of life. Each day we are faced with many decisions that will determine how we spend our time. This is a constant battle that we never really seem to master. Even as a pastor who is supposed to be an example to my church, I struggle constantly in my own life to ensure that I spend valuable time with Jesus Christ. Without that time I am nothing, and my priorities will go more and more astray.

In the days following Dad's death, the words I had read in that email from Ergun Caner came to mind day after day. The theme of "Not I, but Christ" would invade my heart, persistently creeping into virtually every thought and into almost every conversation. It was an all-encompassing concept that I was just starting to comprehend in the early days of my new ministry as pastor. I was only beginning to understand the freedom those words offered to me. I also was starting to open my eyes to the many things that cluttered my life and threatened to keep me from meditating on that truth. I was fully engaged in ministry and fully engaged with my family. I was focusing on all of the important things that were now my responsibility. I was also drowning in grief, still burdened by the incredible loss I felt.

I began to realize that all of these areas of life were choking out the really important thing: the power and presence of God—the cloud of his presence. Sure, I was actively involved in ministry and serving in a large church. Yes, lives were being changed on a daily basis, and our church was impacting Central Virginia in ways I'd never dreamed possible. But I wasn't being changed on a daily basis. I wasn't allowing God's presence to transform me. I came face-to-face with my own faults in preventing God from being able to fully bless me and work in my life.

Sometimes we are forced to confront our weaknesses and address the issues that are holding back the cloud of God's presence from our lives. But we cannot do this until we are willing to place the comparatively insignificant things of life on the back burner and move the things of eternal significance to the forefront. How do we ensure that the "stuff" of life doesn't get in the way? How do we stay focused on the critical things and not on the things that only seem important because they scream loudly for our attention? These are critical questions that I'm sure you have asked yourself on many occasions. We all make promises to spend less time doing trivial things. We even make sincere efforts. Yet how quickly we revert to our old habits. We want to incorporate "Not I, but Christ" into our lives, but in our humanity we struggle to keep that simple and wonderful concept at work in our hearts. We must identify the stuff in our lives that is preventing Christ from being our all in all. Then we must cast our cares on the One who can keep our minds on him.

What are the stumbling blocks in our lives that keep us from focusing properly on God's priorities rather than lamely setting our own? We know that only when we put God first can we fully tap into the power God promises to give us. But somehow we allow far lesser goals and tasks to distract us and derail our quest for what God has planned for us. In this chapter I want to identify some of those misplaced priorities that distract us and prevent us from experiencing the fullness of Christ in our lives. And I'll share some things I've recently learned about how we can let God triumph over our weaknesses and fully work through us.

Mismanaging Time

PROPERLY APPORTIONING our limited time is perhaps more difficult than keeping right priorities in any other area of our lives. "Lack of time" often becomes our stumbling block. Usually because of our own poor planning, we're frequently trying to find more time in our lives: time for family, time for friends, time for hobbies, time for daily Bible study and prayer, time for ministry. When we factor in the time spent at work, eating, sleeping, commuting, and other daily activities, the hours seem to just disappear. We begin to feel the squeeze of time . . . along with the resulting stress. And stress can keep us from realizing our full potential.

When anxiety takes hold in our lives, it hinders our ability to properly experience God's power. God wants us to focus solely on him, even when we are knee-deep in our greatest challenges. Look upward, not inward. I have seen firsthand that when we are facing our greatest trials, God will do his greatest work within us.

Self-Seeking Pride

ANOTHER PRIORITY in our lives that can easily get skewed: who's number one? Who runs the show, gets top billing? Whom is it most important for us to please and honor: God, other people, or ourselves? If the answer is ourselves, that's pride. I believe pride is the single greatest destructive force in most lives. Proverbs 29:23 says, "Pride ends in humiliation, while humility brings honor." Pride is harmful in the life of any believer. Yet we all, including me, have areas of pride that prevent us from fully living out the one great truth, "Not I, but Christ." If we are full of ourselves, we have no room left for Christ.

Usually pride begins creeping into our lives when we start to have a little success, just like my friend whom I spoke of earlier in this chapter. We start making progress in our careers, for example, and receive praise from others for our good work. We start to believe the good things being said about us. In fact, we believe them so much that we magnify those comments in our own minds. We begin to bask in our self-perceived greatness. Pretty soon we believe in our hearts that we are far more important and far more capable than we really are. This is often how pride festers within us. I don't think most people ever intend to become prideful; they simply allow their emotions to reign in their lives. And when pride comes in, "Not I, but Christ" takes a backseat.

Proverbs 16:18 says, "Pride goes before destruction, and haughtiness before a fall." Do we need any clearer picture of what our own pride will bring us? If we are to live victorious lives that honor Jesus Christ, we must empty our hearts of pride to make room for more of God. Pride and self-sufficiency will never lead to success. Only our honesty, humility, and total dependence on Jesus Christ will bring victory and honor.

Not long ago a woman in our church came to see me. Her marriage was falling apart. She shared the story of how she had come to this place in her life, weeping as she told of her husband's verbal abuse, dishonesty, and unfaithfulness. She asked me how someone could fall so far away from God. She wanted answers that could help her understand this tragic situation.

From what she told me, it seemed her husband had begun believing he was somebody important. He had allowed himself to believe that he was capable of making his own decisions, of determining his own destiny, and of building his own future. And with that belief, his dependency on God quickly vanished, leaving his marriage in shambles. He had bought into the tragic lies that he didn't need anyone else and that he didn't make mistakes. He believed that his personal needs and desires were more important than the needs and desires of his family. Nothing good can come from that mind-set.

What words of encouragement can you offer to someone going through what this woman was experiencing? I thought of the words that had helped me get through that first Sunday sermon after my dad's death: "Not I, but Christ." That's the only answer I can give that holds any value. I told her that Christ would bring her through this situation. I told her that Christ is faithful, that his promises are everlasting. I told her that in her weakness he would be strong.

Don't think only those who aren't in tune with God fall into pride. Pride is a danger in all our lives—even, and maybe even especially, in pastors. After I became the senior pastor at Thomas Road Baptist Church, our congregation began growing rapidly, with fifty to sixty people becoming members each Sunday for the first few weeks. This amazed our members and amazed me too. People began sending me emails, calling me, and stopping me after services and at various places around town to tell me what an amazing job I was doing. They praised my sermons. They told me how proud they were of me. They told me how proud Dad would have been to know that I was carrying on his dream.

Unfortunately, I began to believe these people. They were trying to lift me up, but I allowed their positive words to lead to pride that tore me down. I had accepted their words with the wrong spirit. Fortunately, I began to realize this problem, and I quickly determined that I could not permit such comments to go to my head. I had already proclaimed "Not I, but Christ" to the world. I had plastered that one great truth on the walls of our church and had uttered it over and over in my sermons, which were broadcast throughout the nation on television and radio. I quoted those words at every turn. Yet I was struggling to live by them. I knew I had to let this truth sink still deeper into my heart and soul.

I committed this area of my life to God through constant prayer, asking him to deliver me from my own spirit of pride. Boy, did I pray! I knew that to remain grounded in the truth that had gotten me through those tough initial days following Dad's death, I had to continue depending on the One who had given me that strength. Our human nature will always take us in the wrong direction: away from God. It will always drive us away from a simple and utter dependence on him. This is Satan's way of building a barrier between us and God. He knows he cannot move God away from us; but he also knows he can draw us away from God. I believe he targets our sense of pride in order to accomplish this task.

Away from God is a place I have no desire to go. And so, as I began waging this war against pride, I had to make sure that I would not allow it to rear its ugly head in my heart. I knew that if I allowed pride to creep in, the power of God's presence would begin to disappear. Conquering my pride through prayer and dependence on Jesus Christ has become a daily battle.

This battle against pride is an important aspect of seeing God work in your life too. Until we accept this reality, living the life we are intended to live will be impossible. The one great truth of God's power will be absent, and we'll be aimlessly trying to navigate life on our own.

Materialism

MATERIALISM IS another common stumbling block to living a life based solidly on God's priorities rather than our own. We live in a world that is fixated on "things." I believe this quest to have the best of everything is quietly destroying our culture. But this is nothing new. It's human nature to crave more, and such craving is both destructive and ancient. The children of Israel were not exempt from its influence.

When God had given Joshua and the army of Israel victory over the city of Jericho, he gave one specific instruction: all the riches and goods of the city were to be devoted to the Lord and, as such, were totally off-limits to the conquering army. Joshua warned the people: "Keep away from the devoted things, so that you will not bring about your own destruction by taking any of them. Otherwise you will make the camp of Israel liable to destruction and bring trouble on it. All the silver and gold and the articles of bronze and iron are sacred to the LORD and must go into his treasury" (Joshua 6:18–19 NIV). God wasn't being stingy. The instruction was for the people's own good. He knew the dangers we reap when we sow the seeds of materialism in our hearts.

But a man named Achan put his own desire for beautiful and valuable things ahead of honoring and obeying God. Achan stole for himself goods from the plunder that were to be dedicated to the Lord: a beautiful Babylonian robe, two hundred silver coins, and a bar of gold.

The Bible is not saying that having or wanting beautiful clothes, possessions, or money is inherently wrong. But we must be careful to keep our priorities right. We must never allow ourselves to want these things so much that we'll do anything necessary to get them or, like Achan, steal from what rightfully belongs to God—resources or affection that should be devoted to him alone.

Achan's materialism had tragic consequences not only for himself and his family (they were stoned to death, according to Joshua 7:25) but also for the entire nation of Israel. Because Achan put his own desires ahead of obeying God, God was not with Israel, helping them, when they next needed him. Defeating the tiny city of Ai should have been easy, but Ai defeated Israel. Thirty-six men were killed as a direct consequence of Achan's sin, and the rest were forced to retreat in defeat and fear.

Materialism—making wealth or things our priority instead of God, keeping for ourselves resources that should be devoted to God—will destroy a life, a community, or a church. The rapid increase of debt that families are saddled with is ripping the fabric of our nation. And the vast majority of that debt is for items we purchase for no other reason than to enhance our lifestyles. Sure, we need to borrow money occasionally, usually for the purchase of a home or car; but we must be careful not to borrow simply to enhance our social standing or to have more gadgets and toys. Some people are so deeply in debt that they feel as if they're being choked. The joy that once was in their lives is quickly disappearing as a result of the immense pressure of debt. For people to tap into the power of God in their lives, it is imperative that they be free of the crippling effects of materialism.

The insatiable desire to keep up with the neighbors is affecting our lives and our families in terrible ways. I always tell those who discuss these types of situations with me that it is crucial for them to devise a plan to get out of debt and to discontinue the lifestyle choices that brought them to this place. The reason that's so important is this: when we are crippled by debt, we naturally will be distracted from the priority of putting God first. Making or having money will become our top priority, consuming our thoughts, our emotions, our desires, and our time. The simple truth "Not I, but Christ" will always be shoved to the back of the bus when materialism is preeminent in our lives.

There are other forms of slavery to materialism. I know people who have plenty of personal resources and a good income that affords them the ability to pay for whatever they wish to buy. Many of these people are drowning in their own materialism and facing a crisis of faith just as damaging as those who are buried in debt. The Bible doesn't pull any punches when it comes to personal greed: "The love of money is the root of all kinds of evil" (1 Timothy 6:10). The love of money and all that entails can destroy us. Just as the person who is enslaved by debt cannot fully experience God's power, so the person who is captivated by the love of money is similarly hindered in his or her walk with Christ. When money, wealth, and material goods are overly important to us, we have dangerously chosen our own priorities, not God's.

Certainly, many other things in life can keep us from tapping into the power God wants to freely give us, but these two (needless debt and heedless greed) seem to be the ones that do the most damage. Thus it is important that we examine our hearts for any misplaced priorities. Allowing ourselves to get too busy, so that our schedules are out of control or control us; being full of ourselves; being consumed with having or getting material things—all of these will keep us from experiencing the amazing life God has planned for us.

Is it important to have "things" to be happy? No. Is it important to have others lift us up on a pedestal? No. Is it important to focus solely on our work at the expense of our time with God and with our families? Again, no. All of these things will serve as inadequate and fleeting substitutes for God's best in our lives. While we may find a period of enjoyment in temporal activities that separate us from God, I can assure you the enjoyment will be short-lived. At some point these trivial things will lose their luster, and the hunger for a touch from God will overwhelm you. That's when you'll realize that it's not your priorities, but God's, that will bring fulfillment. The key to being successful—in this life and the next—is to value what God values and to live our lives accordingly.

THE IMPORTANCE of having priorities is simple. Some things are *prior* or before other things. My dad wore a lapel pin every day of his life and it was a simple statement—"Jesus First." His relationship with God was first and next was his relationship with his family. This is the nature of priorities. If we keep God first, that will help us to maintain a balance in the other priorities in our lives. When we take our eyes off God, then we are not too far away from having misplaced priorities. Misplaced priorities will always lead to heartache and pain.

QUESTIONS TO CONSIDER

1. Can you remember a time when your priorities got out of sequence? How did you feel?
2. When you neglect spending time with God, how does that affect your life?
3. When you spend time in God's word and time in prayer, how do you feel?
4. How can you make spending time with God a priority?

UPWARD LOOK:

Dear God, thank you for establishing priorities in my life. Thank you for the joy and fulfillment that comes when I follow your plan for my life. Help me to not seek after temporal things like materialism, greed, and selfish pursuits. Help me, instead, to seek the things that will be eternal fulfillment. In Jesus' name, amen.

9

Not My Perfection,
but Christ's

THE ROOF LEAKS. Your loved one is dying. Finances are tight. Your boss is pressuring you to cook the books or lose your job. Your kids are rebelling. Are we having fun yet?

Your neighbor has it in for you. You're getting older, and you just spent your retirement nest egg on medical bills. Your church is in danger of splitting. Your sister refuses to speak to you. You're reviled for your godly lifestyle. Rejoice.

Come again?

That's right, rejoice. "Count it all joy when you fall into various trials" (James 1:2 NKJV).

Does James mean that my father's death should have made me

feel joyful instead of sad? It doesn't feel joyous to lose someone you admire, respect, love, and need so much; it feels terrible.

But James wasn't out of touch or callous. He was looking beyond the trials to the blessings those trials can bring to believers' lives. Here's how James explains it, as translated in *The Message*: "Consider it a sheer gift, friends, when tests and challenges come at you from all sides. You know that under pressure, your faith-life is forced into the open and shows its true colors. So don't try to get out of anything prematurely. Let it do its work so you become mature and well-developed, not deficient in any way" (1:2–4). The *New King James Version* describes the end result of a believer's trials as becoming "perfect and complete, lacking nothing" (verse 4).

If you don't feel perfect and complete, if the prospect of lacking nothing sounds appealing to you, then stop looking at the trials you're facing as curses, plagues, or unfair punishment from God, and start looking at them as opportunities for growth, chances to prove and show your mettle, and fertile ground for maturing into the image of Christ. Humanly speaking, we can't be perfect, but Christ can perfect us through his atoning death on the cross. Hebrews 10:14 says: "It was a perfect sacrifice by a perfect person to perfect some very imperfect people" (MSG). Something good can come out of suffering. I've learned in the past year that God uses trials and difficulties to refine and perfect us. I guess that shouldn't surprise me. After all, it's not my perfection, but Christ's.

The book of James has just five chapters and 108 verses, but in this little book are fifty-four imperatives/commands/encouragements that give us practical wisdom for daily living. Written only about fifteen years after the death and resurrection of Jesus, the book of James was, in fact, the first New Testament book written. At that time Christians were enduring terrible persecution for their faith, so they wanted to know how the Scriptures and Christ related to their lives in practical terms. In essence, they were asking, What does the Word of God offer to help us through our troubles? They needed some practical advice and some tangible words of wisdom that could carry them through this time of intense persecution. If you want to read about what they were enduring, read chapters 8–12 in the book of Acts.

James supplied their answer. The theme of his message is this: faith in Christ will produce works for his glory. We find within this wonderful book soul-enriching words that show us how to live victoriously even when the challenges of life are bearing down on us. Here's some of what James teaches that will help you when you walk through dark valleys of testing.

Trials Produce Patience

JAMES LIKENS patience to the idea of being content as you endure what God allows to come into your life. Sometimes in life we become impatient—we want immediate answers, and according to our own preconceived ideas, when we approach God—and we miss out on the fullest blessing that God intends for us. Our consumer mind-set of "I want it now, and I want it fast" seeps into our Christian life on occasion, and I believe that's damaging. We tend to lack the ability (or even the desire) to be content as we endure the trials and persecution we may face. But because God is all-wise, all-powerful, and never-changing, he always knows what is best for us. Having everything now, when we want it, may not be the best thing for us. Often we must wait and endure difficulties to show the strength of our faith and build the spiritual stamina we'll need for the future. Here are four reflections that have brought me comfort as I've struggled to patiently endure the trials in my own life.

Life Is Not Easy

WELL, THERE'S a news flash. We all have personal stories, firsthand knowledge of life's difficulties. But let's examine what James has to say about trying times. Notice that he said "*When* you fall into various trials" (1:2 NKJV, emphasis added). He didn't say "*If* you fall." We are, indeed, going to face trials in life; there's no avoiding them.

Even though Joshua and the people of Israel were chosen by God and walking in his will, they still faced difficulties and hardships. They had to confront the swollen Jordan River, fight the army of Jericho once the wall fell, and defeat the enemies of Israel in battle after battle to win the land God was giving them. When we follow Jesus Christ, life does not become a bed of roses. In fact, I believe Satan specifically targets believers and constantly brings new temptations into our lives because he wants to defeat us. Further, in our nation Christians often face laughter or ridicule because of their faith in Jesus Christ. It's hard to tolerate. In many lands, however, persecution carries far graver consequences. Our fellow brothers and sisters in Christ regularly face unjust jail sentences, beatings, and even death solely because they have placed their faith in the Son of the living God. I mention this to note that faith in Christ often carries consequences and to reinforce the fact that believers will certainly face trials.

We have no promise of tomorrow, nor do we have any promise that tomorrow will not bring trouble. I frequently tell new believers that they should expect life to get a little harder, rather than easier, in the early days of their new life in Christ. But I also encourage them to take heart, because no matter what hardship comes their way, they have a loving God (as well as godly friends) in their lives to walk with them through difficult times. If we can learn to endure in Christ, we will have a testimony that can be a powerful tool for evangelism and for encouragement of other Christians. People will look at us and glorify God because of our enduring faith. And we will see that it is a privilege to bring honor to Christ through our suffering.

Our Trials Have a Purpose

HAVING TO cross an impossibly swollen Jordan River with God's miraculous help served an important purpose in Joshua's development as a leader: "That day the LORD made Joshua a great leader in the eyes of all the Israelites, and for the rest of his life they revered him as much as they had revered Moses" (Joshua 4:14).

Couldn't God have miraculously emptied the Promised Land for his people so they wouldn't have had to fight so many battles? Of course. But God had good reasons for not giving the people the land all at once. Early on, God told Moses of his plan to handle the people living in the land: "I will not drive them out in a single year, because the land would become desolate and the wild animals would multiply and threaten you. I will drive them out a little at a time until your population has increased enough to take possession of the land" (Exodus 23:29–30).

In Judges 3:1–4 several additional reasons are revealed for the Israelites' having to battle their way gradually into the land of promise. We're told that the Lord left some of Israel's enemies "to teach warfare to generations of Israelites who had no experience in battle" (verse 2) and that "these people were left to test the Israelites—to see whether they would obey the commands the LORD had given to their ancestors through Moses" (verse 4). Our struggles and our difficulties are rites of passage, times of testing designed to bring growth and maturity.

Let's examine the phrase "knowing that the testing of your faith produces patience" (James 1:3 NKJV). The word for "testing" comes from the Greek word *dokimazo* (dok-ee-MAHD-zo) and is always used in the Bible to describe a challenge or situation that provides an opportunity for the recipient to prove himself or herself. The word is always spoken in terms of a positive thing that happens to us. What's interesting is that this same word for "testing" was used to describe the refining process of metals. In the first century, metals such as gold would be heated until they reached liquid form. All the impurities from within the gold would rise to the top in the fiery vat, where they could be skimmed off. The cleansed metals were then allowed to cool. This process made the precious metal even more valuable, since no impurities remained to detract from its worth. The word that refers to the action of skimming off the impurities is the same word used here in James 1:3, which is translated "testing."

We can draw a spiritual conclusion from this cleansing action. We, as believers in Jesus Christ, should accept trials in our lives as God's agents to purify us, helping us to grow in our faith and to come through the "refining fire" as shining examples of God's glory and power. In periods of tribulation, our souls are going through a purification process so that our value in Christ can be at its peak. Our inclination might be to jump out of the fire, but we must remember the truth of this passage and allow God to work his purifying ways in our lives.

Our trials also can serve the purpose of drawing people to Christ. In 2 Timothy 2:10 Paul states, "I am willing to endure anything if it will bring salvation and eternal glory in Christ Jesus to those God has chosen." And as Paul adds in verses 11–12, there are personal benefits to enduring trials with faith in Christ: "This is a trustworthy saying: If we die with him, we will also live with him. If we endure hardship, we will reign with him."

You Don't Need to Worry

MOSES WAS dead, and it was up to Joshua to lead two million Israelites into a land filled with hostile enemies. Not to worry. "Do not be afraid or discouraged," God told Joshua (Joshua 1:9). Overconfident Israel had been badly defeated by tiny Ai, and now they were about to battle them again. Still, no need to worry: "The LORD said to Joshua, 'Do not be afraid or discouraged' " (Joshua 8:1). When you're following God, depending on him to lead and help you, there isn't a problem or difficulty or challenge you can face that is big enough to be worth worrying about. God is always greater. God is always with you. God is always working. Now that's reason for joy!

Let's consider the phrase "count it all joy" (James 1:2). On a recent trip to the West Coast, I spent some time with a successful businessman. We were talking about trials and how we handle these tough periods that often come into our lives. He shared with me that his prayer life is now made up of about 98 percent praise to God due to the great experiences God has brought him through. This type of praying is "count it all joy" in practice. This man didn't focus on his problems when he prayed. Instead, he focused on giving praise to God no matter what he was facing in life.

In John 16:33 Jesus said, "I have told you all this so that you may have peace in me. Here on earth you will have many trials and sorrows. But take heart, because I have overcome the world." I know the heart wants to say, "God, please remove this problem from me!" That's our natural inclination. But knowing that God will always be there to comfort us, we can simply turn our attention to praising him and know that he is at work in our lives.

The apostle Paul reminds us of his own struggles in 2 Corinthians 12:8–10, and the trials he endured relate to our own challenges today. Notice his words: "Three different times I begged the Lord to take it [an unnamed trouble that Paul regularly faced] away. Each time he said, 'My grace is all you need. My power works best in weakness.' So now I am glad to boast about my weaknesses, so that the power of Christ can work through me. That's why I take pleasure in my weaknesses, and in the insults, hardships, persecutions, and troubles that I suffer for Christ. For when I am weak, then I am strong."

Have you ever been there? Have you ever called out to God and pleaded with him to take away a particular burden? We, like Paul, must come to realize that through our afflictions we have the opportunity to rely on God's grace and to experience his magnificent presence in our lives. Instead of being consumed by worry about our afflictions, we must allow God to complete his work in us.

You Can Count on God

GOD DOESN'T just tell us not to worry about our troubles and then not back it up with his promises. He backed up his command to Joshua not to worry or be afraid with a powerful promise: "I will not fail you or abandon you" (Joshua 1:5). Joshua could count on God no matter what he faced. The good news is, so can you and I.

In John 14:1 we read: "Don't let your hearts be troubled. Trust in God, and trust also in me." Jesus spoke these words to the Twelve so that they could experience his wondrous peace and comfort in their lives. The amazing thing about this passage, in my mind, is that just twenty-four hours from the time Jesus made this statement, he would be hanging on the cross, taking on the appalling sins of the world and experiencing physical and emotional pain that we cannot comprehend. With full knowledge that this was his divinely inspired destiny, Jesus was concerned more about his friends than he was about himself. He took the time to make it clear to them that they could trust him and trust God. That is the same Jesus who lives in our hearts, dear friends. He is more concerned with his children than with anything else.

This passage shows the amazing heart of God. In essence, God is telling us that nothing can prevent him from ministering to us in our time of need. What a wonderful promise this is to believers!

First Peter 1:6–7 assures us: "There is wonderful joy ahead, even though you have to endure many trials for a little while. These trials will show that your faith is genuine. It is being tested as fire tests and purifies gold—though your faith is far more precious than mere gold. So when your faith remains strong through many trials, it will bring you much praise and glory and honor on the day when Jesus Christ is revealed to the whole world."

Here's an imperative point that we must remember as we go through trials: God will never tempt us (see James 1:13–15). He will never allow us to go through trials in an effort to make us fall or fail. He doesn't want to see us crash and burn, and he gets no enjoyment out of our struggles. Rather, God empowers us to endure trials so that, with his extraordinary help, we can have incredible victory after victory in life. We can see the hidden beauty in suffering: God's art of making us the purest of vessels, vessels he can used in incredible ways.

―――――――

WHEN WE endure life's trials by clinging to the promises of God, we will be empowered in our walk with Christ. Here are three guarantees God gives us when we choose to endure:

1. Patience Perfects Us

LET'S RETURN our focus to James 1:4: "Let patience have its perfect work, that you may be perfect and complete, lacking nothing" (NKJV). The word *perfect* here refers to maturing. We mature in our faith when we are patient and wait on God. Again, this is not easy for us humans to do. It is not in our nature to wait, even for God. But when we wait on God and place our full trust in him, we often find ourselves thrust to our knees and offering our praises to the One who knows our every need. We are perfected through these experiences and subsequently enjoy our most intimate moments with God.

2. Patience Completes Us

ONE SCENE from the movie *Jerry Maguire* has become famous: the title character, in a soul-bearing moment, tells his wife, "You complete me." But the completion of which he spoke cannot compare to our being completed through the work of Christ. The word *complete* in the first chapter of James means "whole," "well," or "physical or spiritual well-being." This word is often used to describe the people Jesus healed when he walked the earth.

The meaning is further explained in James 1:12, when the author states, "God blesses those who patiently endure testing and temptation. Afterward they will receive the crown of life that God has promised to those who love him." In other words, God allows us to traverse a challenging road in life, all the while guaranteeing that if we allow him to work in us, he will make sure we finish well. Waiting on God during trials is a rite of passage in the Christian life, and it leads to our ultimate completeness in Christ. It will do nothing but make us better for the future.

3. Patience Prepares Us

OUR PATIENT endurance of trials prepares us for even greater things that God has planned for us. As Paul explains it, "There's more to come: We continue to shout our praise even when we're hemmed in with troubles, because we know how troubles can develop passionate patience in us, and how that patience in turn forges the tempered steel of virtue, keeping us alert for whatever God will do next. In alert expectancy such as this, we're never left feeling shortchanged. Quite the contrary—we can't round up enough containers to hold everything God generously pours into our lives through the Holy Spirit!" (Romans 5:3–5 MSG).

———————

SO NOW we understand that God allows trials and troubles in the lives of believers to test, refine, prepare, and perfect us. In spite of our human nature to try to avoid or escape difficult times, our spiritual nature understands that it's important not to "try to get out of anything prematurely" but to "let it do its work" so we will "become mature and well-developed, not deficient in any way" (James 1:4 MSG).

But when we're in the midst of mind-boggling, crushing difficulties, how can we even know how to appropriately respond and act in order to allow this kind of perfecting to take place in our lives? How does God want us to react? If we knew, we'd do it. But often the path seems murky; multiple choices seem equally ineffective. The answer seems hidden. So how can we know what to do and keep from wasting the opportunity for good that could come from the difficulties we're made to endure?

We can ask God.

God Gives Wisdom for Our Trials When We Ask Him

JAMES ASSURES us that God is able and willing to give us the wisdom we need to navigate our troubles in a way that brings glory to him and makes us perfect in Christ. "If any of you lacks wisdom, let him ask of God, who gives to all liberally and without reproach, and it will be given to him" (James 1:5 NKJV). The way it's stated in *The Message* may connect even more with how you feel in the midst of your struggles: "If you don't know what you're doing, pray to the Father. He loves to help."

It's that simple. All we have to do is ask.

When we try to figure out the best course of action based on our own wisdom, we often make the wrong choice—sometimes with devastating, irrevocable consequences. That's because what we know is limited. We can't predict the future. No matter how hard we try, we can't know all the facts. We can't always trust our senses or what we think we see. Plus, there are times when other people intentionally work to deceive us or manipulate our actions in their own favor but to our detriment. Joshua 9 is a perfect illustration of this.

Fearing destruction at the hands of Israel, the people of the city-state of Gibeon resorted to a ruse to save themselves. It was common knowledge that God had strongly warned Joshua not to make any treaties with the people who lived nearby. So the Gibeonites went to great lengths to make it look like they were from a faraway land when they sent ambassadors to ask for a peace treaty with Israel. "They sent ambassadors to Joshua, loading their donkeys with weathered saddlebags and old, patched wineskins. They put on worn-out, patched sandals and ragged clothes. And the bread they took with them was dry and moldy. When they arrived at the camp of Israel at Gilgal, they told Joshua and the men of Israel, 'We have come from a distant land to ask you to make a peace treaty with us' " (Joshua 9:4–6).

Joshua and the people of Israel weren't totally gullible. They recognized that things might not be exactly as presented. They asked, "How do we know you don't live nearby? For if you do, we cannot make a treaty with you" (Joshua 9:7).

But a little flattery and skillful avoidance seemed to be all the Gibeonites needed to give the Israelites a false sense of security.

> Your servants have come from a very distant country. We have heard of the might of the LORD your God and of all he did in Egypt. . . .
> This bread was hot from the ovens when we left our homes. But now, as you can see, it is dry and moldy. These wineskins were new when we filled them, but now they are old and split open. And our clothing and sandals are worn out from our very long journey. (Joshua 9:9–13)

The account was believable. The men's condition appeared to validate their story. The only way the Israelites could have known that a peace treaty was the wrong thing to do was to ask God what he wanted them to do. They'd done it before when they didn't know what to do next (see Joshua 7:6–9). But this time they thought they could make the right decision on their own. "The Israelites examined their food, but they did not consult the LORD" (Joshua 9:14).

They made a treaty with the Gibeonites, disobeying God's direct command with tragic consequences that began just a short time later, with war to defend Gibeon, and stretched all the way to the time of Saul and David (see 2 Samuel 21). All because Joshua and the

Israelites failed to recognize their need to ask God for wisdom. We need not make the same mistake. God wants us to ask him for wisdom in the midst of our struggles. Let's look more closely at what James tells us about asking for God's wisdom.

We Have an Open Invitation

JAMES 1:5 says, "If any of you . . ." (NKJV) God's wisdom is available to *all* his children, but we must sense the need, ask for help, and willingly receive it. Wisdom, like patience, is not applied to our lives just because we're born. But this promise is applicable to everyone who believes on Jesus Christ for salvation and spiritual security.

Some Application Is Required

WE NEED to realize that while God is the source of our strength, he will not force himself on us. We must choose to seek his will and his power in our lives.

When Jesus selected the Twelve, he gave them power and authority to do miraculous things in his name. Matthew 10:1 tells us, "Jesus called his twelve disciples together and gave them authority to cast out evil spirits and to heal every kind of disease and illness." So we see that they had authority and power. But here's the important question regarding this heavenly strength that was afforded them: would they always be victorious in overcoming the challenges they faced because of this power?

The answer is no. Notice this account in Matthew 17:14–21, where we read of the disciples' failure:

> At the foot of the mountain, a large crowd was waiting
> for them. A man came and knelt before Jesus and said,
> "Lord, have mercy on my son. He has seizures and suffers

terribly. He often falls into the fire or into the water. So I brought him to your disciples, but they couldn't heal him."

Jesus said, "You faithless and corrupt people! How long must I be with you? How long must I put up with you? Bring the boy here to me." Then Jesus rebuked the demon in the boy, and it left him. From that moment the boy was well.

Afterward the disciples asked Jesus privately, "Why couldn't we cast out that demon?"

"You don't have enough faith," Jesus told them. "I tell you the truth, if you had faith even as small as a mustard seed, you could say to this mountain, 'Move from here to there,' and it would move. Nothing would be impossible."

God provides power, but it's up to us to strengthen our belief in him. Only in strong faith can we experience great power.

We Must Make the Request

"IF ANY of you lacks wisdom, let him ask of God" (James 1:5 NKJV). The word *ask* should be understood as a continual asking or constant request. In fact, this phrase could be translated, "let him continually be asking God." We should be engaged in a never-ending series of requests, asking God to light our path, guide our steps, and work within us so that we may bring honor and glory to him. Our weakness can be transformed into strength when we are persistent in seeking God's wisdom for every aspect of our lives.

We Have God's Promise

"IF ANY of you lacks wisdom, let him ask of God, who gives to all liberally and without reproach, and it will be given to him" (James 1:5 NKJV). If we are willing to daily, continually ask for wisdom, God will give it to us. Notice two qualities of this promise:

- God will give liberally. The word *liberally* is used not only in James 1:5 but (as *liberality*) also in 2 Corinthians 8 (to describe how the Macedonian churches gave to help others in need) and 2 Corinthians 9 (to describe how the church of Corinth should sow liberally or generously so they would reap liberally or generously). So we see that this means God will give generously out of an abundance of his riches of wisdom.

- God will give graciously. We see the bountiful grace of God in the phrase "without reproach." This important part of verse 5 shows that God gives to us regardless of our condition, regardless of our status, and regardless of our actions. He finds no fault in us when we come to him needing wisdom and help. Remember, when we pray, God responds to us in the role of our heavenly Father. Like any earthly father, God truly wants the best for his children. He is pleased when we approach him for counsel and guidance. He is even more pleased when we trust in him and live out his design for our lives with the faith of a child.

We Will See Evidence

JAMES 3:13–18 (NIV) says,

> Who is wise and understanding among you? Let him
> show it by his good life, by deeds done in the humility
> that comes from wisdom. But if you harbor bitter envy
> and selfish ambition in your hearts, do not boast about it
> or deny the truth. Such "wisdom" does not come down
> from heaven but is earthly, unspiritual, of the devil. For
> where you have envy and selfish ambition, there you find
> disorder and every evil practice.
>
> But the wisdom that comes from heaven is first of all
> pure; then peace-loving, considerate, submissive, full of
> mercy and good fruit, impartial and sincere. Peacemakers
> who sow in peace raise a harvest of righteousness.

When we face trials, God's wisdom is our power source. God's grace will guide us and allow us to see our defeats turned into great victories. And when we come through our times of testing and people see the power of Christ in our lives, we can then help those people discover their own full potential in Christ.

Wisdom Has a Purpose.

CLEARLY, CULTIVATING wisdom in our lives is for our own benefit. It also brings glory to God. But cultivating wisdom in our lives also benefits those we love. We are to live in the wisdom of God and let it transform our daily actions so that our families, our friends, our neighbors, and everyone with whom we come in contact will be enriched through us. I want to speak especially to families:

Fathers, your family needs a wise dad.

Mothers, your family needs a wise mom.

Children, you need wisdom beyond your years.

Grandparents, you need to share godly wisdom with those who have not yet attained your level of spiritual insight.

In Proverbs 1:20–33 wisdom is personified and calls out, urging people to take heed and not fall into utter ruin because they shun her:

Wisdom shouts in the streets.
> She cries out in the public square.
She calls to the crowds along the main street,
> to those gathered in front of the city gate:
"How long, you simpletons,
> will you insist on being simpleminded?
How long will you mockers relish your mocking?
> How long will you fools hate knowledge?
Come and listen to my counsel.
I'll share my heart with you
> and make you wise.

"I called you so often, but you wouldn't come.
> I reached out to you, but you paid no attention.
You ignored my advice
> and rejected the correction I offered.
So I will laugh when you are in trouble!
> I will mock you when disaster overtakes you—
when calamity overtakes you like a storm,
> when disaster engulfs you like a cyclone,
> and anguish and distress overwhelm you.

"When they cry for help, I will not answer.

Though they anxiously search for me, they will not find me.

For they hated knowledge

and chose not to fear the LORD.

They rejected my advice

and paid no attention when I corrected them.

Therefore, they must eat the bitter fruit of living their own way,

choking on their own schemes.

For simpletons turn away from me—to death.

Fools are destroyed by their own complacency.

But all who listen to me will live in peace,

untroubled by fear of harm."

I know many wise Christians, people who have lived out their lives in service to God with humility and gentleness of spirit. They serve as a great source of encouragement to me and to many others who value their wise and spirit-filled counsel. The heart of a wise Christian is always open to helping people—not in a prideful way but in a manner that desires to help them discover peace and meaning in their Christian walk. These wise Christians gain their insight and influence from the Holy Spirit.

Most churches have a handful of wise counselors who impact their congregations in ways that only God could ordain. Their value is inestimable. As a pastor, I often pray that God will supply our church with more and more of these people. We all should strive to be the kind of believer who can encourage, instruct, and motivate others to follow Christ. Such Christians have tapped into the power of Christ. It is evident in their manner, in their conversation, and in their deeds.

Through Christ we can become that kind of person, and we can impact those around us in ways that will have eternal results. For all who desire them, God's wisdom and power are there for the asking.

———————

GOD USES even the most terrible circumstances to work good. In spite of incomprehensible suffering and tribulation, Joseph of old knew this and learned to joyfully embrace his trials for the good they produced. In forgiving his brothers, he demonstrated wisdom and the perfecting grace God had worked in his life through his patient endurance: "You intended to harm me, but God intended it for good to accomplish what is now being done, the saving of many lives" (Genesis 50:20 NIV).

We, too, can know such perfect wisdom. All we must do is ask. For it is "Not my perfection, but Christ's."

WHEN YOU face a difficult circumstance you must not respond out of the natural, but you need to rely on the supernatural power and promises of the Word of God. When we lash out at a circumstance or a person there is no need for patience. There is no need for wisdom. As a result the process and the end that God has in mind for us doesn't have a chance to materialize.

When we respond to a trial or a test with patience and wisdom then God has a chance to develop in us the life of Christ. It's not easy, but it's worth it because patience in the face of trial produces wisdom. God's wisdom gives us the ability to see and respond to the toughest situation with God's perspective. When we live in this manner we can experience "Not my perfection, but Christ's."

QUESTIONS TO CONSIDER:

1. What has been the toughest trial that you have had to go through?
2. What is the difference between God's wisdom and man's wisdom?
3. Recount a situation in your life when you needed and received wisdom from above.
4. Jonathan stated that "something good can come out of suffering." Has that ever been true in your life? If so, what?

UPWARD LOOK:

Dear God, thank you for the grace and the wisdom that you give me in the midst of trials and suffering. Thank you that even in the midst of suffering, you are teaching me to be patient. Thank you for the wisdom that I receive from your Word and the strength I receive when I read the Bible. I praise you for wanting to make me like your Son, who suffered for me. In Jesus' name, amen.

10

Not My Sand, but God's Rock

Our church has seen God work in amazing ways during the critical months following the death of our leader, my father. The Lord has worked in our congregation despite the doubts I've expressed in myself as a pastor, despite the fact that our members were unsure what would happen in the wake of Dad's death, and despite the fact that the future seemed uncertain when our Moses was called home.

I'm not saying we've all grown into carefree and untroubled people. I'm not even saying that we have a constant, clear vision of what lies in store for us. Of course, God knows what will occur within us as we travel the path of life. He knows how I will respond to the challenges placed before me. But our situation really is no different than the life trials of any believer. Mysteries await us at every turn in life. Yet I know one thing: because of his great power, I am expecting God to perform wonderful, God-size miracles in my life and in the lives of my family. We have determined that we will get out of the way and allow God to build us up for his glory.

We have been striving to live out that one great truth, "Not I, but Christ." We continually offer ourselves as living sacrifices to God. We want to allow the Lord Jesus Christ, the builder of our lives and ministry, to continue empowering us—to be wise Christian stewards, to seek his will in all our efforts, and to respond without question when we discern what he is commanding. If we can continue to do our best to work together in this regard, we can be assured that our lives will be used by him to see folks come to Christ and become a part of the excitement that is taking place within our church.

Further, we can, as individuals, expect to keep running the race, as Paul has described the Christian life, so that when we come to the end of this pursuit, we will enter into God's kingdom knowing that we have given our all for Christ. The members of our church and I are urging God to allow us to jointly and individually live out an audacious faith so that we will one day stand before Christ and be commended as faithful servants.

I tell our members in Lynchburg that if we want to make an impact in our community for God's glory, we must always ensure that we are building our lives and ministries on the proper foundation. I am committed to making sure that the strong spiritual foundation set forth by my father many years ago remains the sturdy groundwork supporting this wonderful church when my days as its pastor are over. I pray daily that everything I do is anchored in the firm foundation that is Jesus Christ. If this remains my fervent prayer, the Lord will enable me to lead these people I have come to love with the humility of spirit and calm confidence that comes to those who wait on God, depend on God, and live for God. These are the qualities we all can embody daily.

Build Your House on the Right Foundation

IN CHAPTER seven of Matthew's gospel, Jesus describes for us the dangers of building our lives on the wrong foundation. In this story that many of us learned as children, we see that the foundation is the basis of everything we do for Christ. The passage reads:

> Whoever hears these sayings of Mine, and does them, I will liken him to a wise man who built his house on the rock: and the rain descended, the floods came, and the winds blew and beat on that house; and it did not fall, for it was founded on the rock.
>
> But everyone who hears these sayings of Mine, and does not do them, will be like a foolish man who built his house on the sand: and the rain descended, the floods came, and the winds blew and beat on that house; and it fell. And great was its fall. (Matthew 7:24–27 NKJV)

Based on this passage, I want to share three important principles that are critical to believers who are attempting to build their lives on spiritual principles that will help them stand firm through good times and bad.

Principle 1: Without the Right Foundation, the House Is Doomed.

NOTICE THAT this passage mentions two types of foundations upon which a person can build: rock and sand. Both of these elements have value, and both are attractive to a property owner. But only one can be trusted as a foundation to sustain us, protect us, and provide permanence. Sand is always shifting; it moves based on the pressure of the wind and waves. We cannot depend on sand to be a foundation that is fixed and durable. Sand will betray us.

The end result of building on sand isn't up for debate. It isn't a matter of odds—maybe it will be reliable, maybe it won't. If you build your life on sand—on anything other than the solid rock of Christ and his Word—the end is certain, and it's not good news: "When the rains and floods come and the winds beat against that house, it will collapse with a mighty crash" (Matthew 7:27).

But the storms of life will not destroy what we build on the Rock: "Though the rain comes in torrents and the floodwaters rise and the winds beat against that house, it won't collapse because it is built on bedrock" (Matthew 7:25).

Every person must choose a foundation upon which to build his or her life. Building on Jesus by following his teachings is the only wise choice.

Principle 2: Knowing Must Lead to Doing.

THE PROBLEM, as made clear in this passage in Matthew, is not that we can't tell what God wants us to do. The teachings in God's Word clearly tell us how to act and live from day to day. The problem instead resides in our hearts. Matthew 7:26 tells us, "Anyone who hears my teaching and doesn't obey it is foolish, like a person who builds a house on sand." When we determine that we will disobey

God, despite his instruction, our lives are destined to career out of control. I have pointed to the need for godly wisdom in our lives. Well, running from God is the epitome of foolishness.

We all have a rebel streak and are inclined to sometimes hear God's Word and pretend it went over our heads, that it doesn't apply to us, or that surely what we're doing qualifies or is good enough. But if we want to live securely in the fullness of Christ, we must be prepared to hear God's Word and accept it with enthusiasm and without reserve. We must move beyond simply *hearing* or *reading* the teachings of Jesus and actually get down to the business of *doing* what he has commanded. As James put it:

> Get rid of all the filth and evil in your lives, and humbly accept the word God has planted in your hearts, for it has the power to save your souls.
> But don't just listen to God's word. You must do what it says. Otherwise, you are only fooling yourselves. (1:21–22)

As Matthew 7:24 tells us, the wise person hears God's words and follows them. If we live our lives in this manner, we will be wise also. What greater honor could there be than to have God examine our hearts and determine that we are wise?

Compare the actions of the wise man to the foolish man in verse 26. The foolish man hears the very same words of God but determines that he has a better plan. The difference between the wise man and the foolish man is not that one of them didn't hear the clear calling of God. The problem was his heart's attitude—he was determined that he couldn't afford to conform to the calling of God. We must continually examine our hearts to ensure that we are not following our own designs for our lives but God's. We must inspect our motives in all that we do so that we can ensure that we are living in the wisdom of God.

Principle 3: Every Life Will Be Put to the Test.

WE OFTEN see in the news how vicious tornadoes, floods, or hurricanes sweep through neighborhoods and, in short order, wipe them out. Homes are torn apart. Likewise, the spiritual lives we build will face onslaughts that put our foundation to the test. Notice in this passage that the identical circumstances struck both the wise man and the foolish man. In fact, the conditions of the storm are described in identical words. For the wise man, who built his house upon the rock, "the rain descended, the floods came, and the winds blew and beat on that house" (Matthew 7:25 NKJV). Just so for the foolish man, who built his house upon the sand, "the rain descended, the floods came, and the winds blew and beat on that house" (Matthew 7:27 NKJV).

When I was a kid, John Cameron Swayze was the pitchman for Timex watches. His catchphrase was, "Timex takes a licking and keeps on ticking." If we value reliability and endurance in something so small and inexpensive as a watch, how much more should we value a steadfast and reliable foundation for our lives? The houses of both wise and foolish builders may look strong as long as the weather is good. But as soon as storms come and the structures are put to the test, the difference in the quality of the foundations becomes quickly apparent.

Oftentimes in life, a crisis will hit us hard, just like a storm. We first see a little "rain" and hope it will carry no lasting consequence. But then that rain becomes a perfect storm of anguish, pain, and distress that floods our hearts and minds. I will tell you from my own experience that when these storms crash upon your life, it's absolutely imperative that you have your spiritual house grounded on a foundation that was built by the unshakable, immovable hand of God. If you have built upon any other foundation, you've built on shifting sand, and you're in for a rough ride.

Proverbs 10:25 emphasizes this point: "When the storms of life come, the wicked are whirled away, but the godly have a lasting foundation." You see, our solid foundation is what keeps us anchored in God's will and within God's protection. We must build our lives, our spiritual houses, on the foundation of the gospel so that when the great storms come, we can be sure that God's mighty hand of protection is there to keep us within his safety and his love.

Beware of Building on Sand

ONLY A fool would choose to build his house on sand. Yet millions of people do this every day with something far more valuable than houses of wood and brick: they do it with their entire lives and eternal souls. It's easy in the natural world to differentiate between sand and rock. But what is the spiritual or philosophical equivalent of sand that is either so difficult to recognize or so appealing that people would willingly choose to build their lives on it rather than on solid rock?

Certainly the various belief systems, religions, or worldviews that are not solidly built on God's Word qualify as sand. But people who incorporate these into their lives have consciously rejected the teachings of Jesus. Yet even those who proclaim themselves Christians and sound and look like believers must be careful lest they find themselves building not on the rock of Christ but upon shifting sand. What are some of these hidden sand traps we must be careful to avoid?

Hidden Sand Trap 1: Good Works

AS YOU look across the religious landscape today, you will find many philosophies that encourage people to build their spiritual houses on the foundation of good works. Such people live their lives based on the hope that doing good to and for others is sufficient by itself to merit salvation and spiritual security. Sometimes called the social gospel, this belief system teaches that the most important thing in life is helping our fellow man—assisting the underprivileged and reaching out to those in need.

Helping others is certainly a responsibility of every person. My father was an excellent example of someone who helped those in need. He knew that it wasn't good enough to speak against the wrongs of this world; we must offer God-honoring alternatives to sinful choices. That's why today our ministry has many outreaches such as the Elim Home (an alternative for alcoholics and drug-addicted men); the Liberty Godparent Home (a facility that gives young, pregnant girls an alternative to abortion); the Family Life Services (an adoption agency that helps the Godparent Home find Christian couples to adopt babies into their homes); Liberty University (the largest evangelical Christian university in America); the Center for Global Ministries (a world outreach and aid ministry that sends Christian high-school and college students around the globe with the message of Christ). We want to help people who are hungry and beleaguered. But we must not lose our focus and place too much emphasis on offering physical help instead of the spiritual solution to their problems. And we must never fall into the trap of believing that our good works mean that we are good enough to meet God's standard. Salvation is through Christ alone. Good works are the fruit of a life saved by God's grace, not the way to that salvation.

Ephesians 2:8–9 emphasizes this point by reminding us: "By

grace you have been saved through faith, and that not of yourselves; it is the gift of God, not of works, lest anyone should boast [that we've done it ourselves]" (NKJV). Titus 3:5 also supports the fact that our spiritual formation is based "not by works of righteousness which we have done, but according to His mercy He saved us, through the washing of regeneration and renewing of the Holy Spirit" (NKJV). We must never lose our focus on elevating Christ. As James 2:14–26 reminds us, the saving grace of Christ produces works. The social gospel inverts this process by suggesting that good works will earn us saving grace.

Hidden Sand Trap 2: Tradition

PERHAPS YOU'VE heard of the family who, for three generations, passed down the secret recipe for a mouthwatering roast that included instructions to cut the narrow end off the meat and nestle it along one of the sides of the pan. Finally, one daughter being entrusted with the special family recipe dared to ask, "Mom, why do we cut the end off the roast?" The mother didn't have an answer, so she asked her mother, who also didn't know. The question was finally asked of the family's ninety-four-year-old matriarch. "Grandmother," the woman asked, "why do you cut the end off your special pot roast?"

The woman answered, "Because all I ever had to cook it in was a tiny little pan that was too short to hold a good-size roast."

Sometimes churches continue cutting the roast in spite of having a new, giant roasting pan—oblivious to the reasons for their actions, heedless of how circumstances have changed, and unwilling to adjust methods and practices to fit the times and the purposes God intends.

Similarly, in our lives, I believe we often hang on to old and tired ideas simply because they worked in the past. We allow bad ideas to stay around a lot longer than they should. "If it ain't broke, don't fix it." But I don't believe we should ever be afraid of discovering new methods of taking the gospel to our fellow humans. In fact, I believe we must be open to finding new methods of reaching new generations of people with the never-changing message of the gospel of Christ.

The Gospel of Mark warns us of the danger of building our spiritual house on tradition rather than on God's instructions: "Jesus replied, 'You hypocrites! Isaiah was right when he prophesied about you, for he wrote, "These people honor me with their lips, but their hearts are far from me. Their worship is a farce, for they teach manmade ideas as commands from God." For you ignore God's law and substitute your own tradition.' Then he said, 'You skillfully sidestep God's law in order to hold on to your own tradition' " (Mark 7:6–9).

Tradition is wonderful in many regards. But if a tradition has become more important than fulfilling our responsibility to live our lives for God and to reach the world with the gospel, we need to be willing to let that tradition die. Don't build your life on traditions, be they family traditions or traditions of the church. Anyone who does will find all he or she has labored to build washed away by the power of life's storms.

Hidden Sand Trap 3: Self-Comfort

LIKE A Burger King order, we often want to have it our way. We don't want to have to adjust, don't want to have to go out of our way, don't want to do without anything we like or think might taste or feel good. Unfortunately, having things our way is a slippery and dangerous foundation on which to build a life.

The "have it your way" philosophy not only invades our hearts, it often invades our families: We become uncomfortable standing up against the sin that creeps into our lives. We avoid the biblical teachings that call attention to our pride and self-centered natures. We even doubt that there's only one way to God, and that's through faith in Jesus Christ and obedience to his teachings. In essence, people who get caught in the shifting sand of self-comfort don't want to feel uncomfortable in the way they live their lives. They don't want to be told that anything they're doing is wrong, unwise, immoral, or sinful. It isn't long until secular ideas are placed on the same level as biblical doctrine.

We cannot afford to ignore Bible truths, even those that sometimes cut into our hearts and make us cringe with awareness of our sinfulness. In 2 Timothy 4:3 Paul warns: "A time is coming when people will no longer listen to sound and wholesome teaching. They will follow their own desires and will look for teachers who will tell them whatever their itching ears want to hear."

I have determined that in my life I will do everything possible to maintain a resolute commitment to the Word of God and to the God of the Word. As long as I am able, and with God's help, I will never sway in my beliefs just because they are more difficult, make me uncomfortable or unpopular within the culture, or teach me that I need to change something in my life. I will preach the Word, just as my father did for more than fifty years. I will build my life on the solid foundation of the teachings of Christ, knowing there is no firm foundation but that one.

Hidden Sand Trap 4: Religiosity

SOME BELIEVERS in Jesus Christ may be tempted to try to impress people with their supersized spirituality, holier-than-thou demeanor, or vast spiritual knowledge. They think that if they look the part of a spiritual person, if they can convince others of how good they are, then surely God will be impressed and convinced too. They want to portray an image of having it all together in their lives. I think this is the result of pride that so easily creeps into our hearts and leads us to draw attention to ourselves and our personal accomplishments. But making the appearance of godliness, or religiosity, the foundation for our lives is a foolish idea. Such a foundation is full of fractures and weaknesses. It tends to be based on ever-changing cultural expectations of godliness rather than on the never-changing Word of God.

In 2 Timothy 3 Paul warned Timothy that in the last days, increasing numbers of people would embrace a form of outward Christianity without having the life-changing power of Christ within. "They will act religious, but they will reject the power that could make them godly. Stay away from people like that!" (2 Timothy 3:5).

Note that I'm not talking about the desire to live lives of excellence. At Thomas Road Baptist Church, we believe and teach that we should pursue excellence in everything we do. As my father always said, "If it's Christian, it ought to be better!" But we are not lost in the trends of the day. We attempt to balance the great traditions of the faith with new methods designed to touch the hearts of people. We want to show the world that our devotion to God is important, and we want everything we do for him to be done with excellence. But that pursuit of excellence has nothing to do with how a certain thing may be perceived by others in the community. Rather, it is based on the desire to do everything we do for God's glory.

When we live our lives based on spiritual excellence, we want others to see that there is, indeed, something different within us. But the purpose is so that others will see Christ within us and will be drawn to him.

Jesus Christ Is the Only Firm Foundation

THE TEACHINGS of Jesus Christ are the only firm foundation upon which we can build our lives and his church. He is the only foundation that can anchor us in truth. Of greater significance, no one and no thing can stand against him or overwhelm someone securely anchored in him. When Peter boldly proclaimed his faith in Jesus as the Christ, the Son of the living God, Jesus assured Peter—and believers today—that he had chosen the firm foundation for his life: "Upon this rock I will build my church, and all the powers of hell will not conquer it" (Matthew 16:18).

When Jesus said he would build his church "upon this rock," he used the word that referred to bedrock. Nothing, absolutely nothing on earth or in the spirit world would ever be able to overcome, defeat, shake, or conquer the church—or the individual life—built securely upon the rock of Jesus Christ. For no other foundation can this claim be made. No other foundation will help us endure when the storms of life pound us. No other foundation can help us resist the temptations of Satan, who seeks to devour us. No other foundation is secure enough to bring us through the trials we face in life in absolute safety and peace.

Years ago a developer in my hometown of Lynchburg purchased a large expanse of land with the intent of establishing a major shopping complex. He had great plans that would have earned him millions of dollars. He was motivated to make it work. But then the excavators of that land hit bedrock. The man spent great amounts of money trying to blast through that rock, but the excavation continued much longer than he had scheduled; he ran out of money and suspended his efforts to build the complex. The bedrock proved to be more powerful than the many dynamite blasts that challenged it. The developer's best efforts were not even close to being enough to shake or break that unyielding foundation of rock.

Against Satan's attacks God is like that bedrock, and then some. Sadly, many people don't want to anchor their lives to the rock of Christ. Rather than building their lives on a firm foundation, they choose shifting sand. They make this choice because they think God demands too much of them. They know that in order to follow him, they must turn their backs on the foundations the world loves. But what these individuals fail to see is that in Christ we have more peace and fulfillment than the world can ever hope to offer. And so the inevitable storms of life come, and because these foolish ones are anchored only to the shifting sands of the world, their foundations are shaken.

Near the end of his lifetime and ministry, Joshua gathered the children of Israel he had led for the many years since the death of their great leader, Moses. He set before them a critical choice: upon what would they build their lives after he was gone? It wasn't enough for Moses, Joshua, or any leader to choose to build upon the rock of God; every individual and family would have to choose for itself: "Fear the LORD and serve him wholeheartedly. Put away forever the idols your ancestors worshiped when they lived beyond the Euphrates River and in Egypt. Serve the LORD alone. But if you refuse to serve the LORD, then choose today whom you will serve. . . . But as for me and my family, we will serve the LORD" (Joshua 24:14–15).

Each of us must make the same choice today. Whom will you serve: God or false gods loved by this world? Upon what foundation will you build your life: the solid Rock or the sands of good works, tradition, self-comfort, religiosity, or any other feel-good philosophy that's in vogue this week? You can't make any foundation safe and secure, no matter how hard you try. There is no firm foundation but God's. Choose it. Choose life. Choose today.

Some might say that it's arrogant to suggest that there's only one way to build and only one Builder who can sustain us. To them I would respond, with respect and kindness, the words of the apostle Peter: "There is salvation in no one else! God has given no other name under heaven by which we must be saved" (Acts 4:12).

I am anchored to the Rock that will withstand all tests, all trials, and all challenges. And you can build your life on this same foundation. Many distractions in this world threaten to keep us from building on the solid Rock. Like building a home on sandy beachfront property, building our lives on foundations such as good works, tradition, self-comfort, or religiosity may be appealing, but the eventual consequences will be catastrophic. Storms come, winds blow, sands shift, buildings fall, and with them everything we value in life.

But not if you're built on the Rock, the firm foundation, Jesus Christ. I encourage you to remain true to the Rock that will never fail you. Passionately focus on him—the author and finisher of our faith—knowing that only through Christ can we discover true joy and peace. By continuing to live out the formula "Not I, but Christ," we will find ourselves secure, on solid ground through the journeys of life. We will experience the great power that comes from building on the rock that is Jesus Christ.

BY CONTINUING to live out the formula "Not I, but Christ," you will find an inner peace in the midst of the storm. You will experience the great power that comes from building on the rock that is Jesus Christ.

QUESTIONS TO CONSIDER:

1. What sand traps have you fallen for in the past? (Good works, traditions, self-comfort, religiosity?)
2. How firm is the foundation for your life right now?
3. Jesus Christ is the only firm foundation for life. What events led up to your decision to make Jesus the only foundation for your life?
4. If Jesus is not the only foundation for your life, make sure you settle this important question right now.

UPWARD LOOK:

Dear God, thank you for sending Jesus to this earth to die on the cross for the sins of the whole world. Thank you that when I place my trust in him, I can receive not only eternal life, but also a firm foundation for this life. In Jesus' name, amen.

11

Not My Effort, but God's Gift

I N   T H E   W E E K S   and months following Dad's death, many
people came to know Christ as Savior. Hundreds of people
walked the aisles to the front of the church, giving their hearts
and lives to Christ. I had never imagined how much joy that would
bring to a pastor's heart. Certainly I had rejoiced in times past over
people coming to know the Lord, but now it had taken on a brand-
new meaning. After the great trial of losing our Moses, God was
graciously pouring out his blessings on us.

The fact that the God of salvation works uniquely in our lives
during times of terrible trial is what gave me stability in the most tur-
bulent time of my life. I saw God distinctively working in my life

during those rough days as I began to anchor my life more deeply into his firm foundation. And that solid ground has kept me propped up in the midst of storms that have arisen in my life since that time. Without my faith in my Lord Jesus Christ, I would feel as if I were on a drifting raft, tossed about uncontrollably on the sea of life.

I believe that experiencing God's comforting touch in my life is what was needed to open my eyes to the spiritual needs of people. The truth that God will provide salvation to any and every lost soul is what will bring those souls peace and stability. And making that truth known should be the driving motivation of every Christian. In the months since Dad's death, I have been reinvigorated in my desire to tell everyone about Jesus. I want them to know the peace that surpasses understanding. I want to encourage my congregation, Liberty University students, and all who watch me on television to be bold and compassionate ambassadors for Christ.

The truth of the gospel drives me to tell others about Jesus. The members of Thomas Road Baptist Church and I have a passion to reach Lynchburg and the neighboring communities with the hope of the gospel. Moreover, we have a zeal to reach the world with the saving knowledge of this gospel. That's why we continue to broadcast our church services and Liberty University convocation services throughout the world. That's why the church and the university send hundreds of students, faculty, and volunteers to a host of nations each year. That's why our church funds dozens of missionaries worldwide. And it's why we train our members to be living testaments to the power of Jesus Christ in their own lives.

I learned this from Dad. You know, I traveled with my father all over the world, and it never failed to amaze me that wherever he went, he seemed to know somebody. I saw him stop to talk to senators and shoeshiners. And I saw him pray with senators and shoeshiners. He was never afraid to talk about Jesus, no matter who a person was.

A man who works for Thomas Road Baptist Church recently told me about a time he was traveling in Amherst County with my father. As they were driving to their destination, Dad noticed a little mom-and-pop store along the side of the road. "Let's stop in here for a minute so I can say hello to a couple of people," he said. They parked and stepped into the old store, which was rundown and scantily stocked. Inside, the old couple who ran the store saw Dad coming through the door and rushed to greet him. "Hello, Jerry!" they both shouted. The man with Dad said that he treated that old couple as if they were royalty. They chatted about folks they had known through the years and about the garden the couple was growing in back of the store. They laughed and reminisced about days gone by in Lynchburg. When it was time to go, Dad said, "Let's have a word of prayer." And there, in that dimly lit old shop on the shore of the James River, Dad shared a simple prayer with that elderly couple. When they returned to the car, Dad said that the two were not Christians, and he didn't want to pass by without visiting and praying with them. What a great example of the desires of my dad's heart. He was a man with great responsibility, but he took none of those responsibilities as seriously as the one to tell others about Christ.

Dad had a true passion for souls. If we don't have a similar passion to reach out to our lost friends, neighbors and loved ones, we really have no reason to even gather together at church every Sunday morning. Sure, we could get together and sing great songs, study some Bible passages, and have a time of fellowship. Those are all important, but Jesus made it clear in Mark 16:15 that the role of Christians is to carry his message to the world: "Go into all the world and preach the Good News to everyone."

We're charged with the responsibility of telling others about Jesus Christ. This is a charge I do not take lightly. We must share the gospel with others, and we must be convinced in our hearts that we should do so at every opportunity. God will give us opportunities, but we must be willing to then step out in faith and talk to people about him. We must get comfortable with sharing our faith and our testimony with people. We must be committed to telling others what Jesus has done in our lives so that they will have a desire to see what he can do in their lives as well.

When we're serious about this assignment that God has given us to tell others about him, we will see results. We'll see people saved and lives transformed. We'll see God at work in amazing ways in our lives and in our churches. And we'll see the pews filled with people who want to know what's going on in churches that recommit to living by the great truth "Not I, but Christ."

For years I had heard my father share the Good News that God provides salvation to all who are willing to accept his free gift of eternal life. Like many seasoned Christians, I could recite all the biblical passages that tell us we are sinners and that Christ came into the world to save those who will repent of their sins and place their trust solely in him. Maybe I actually knew the words too well. The routine had become so familiar that I regularly found myself, while sitting in church, able to predict the next line Dad might say as he urged non-believers in the congregation and those tuning in via television and radio to pray the "sinner's prayer." I watched my father share the salvation message passionately and with ease and confidence time after time through the years. It never became "routine" for Dad. But I think it did for me.

It wasn't until I stepped into Dad's former role at Thomas Road Baptist Church that I realized perhaps I had become desensitized to the seriousness of an altar call or to the importance of explaining the gospel. After Dad's death, it became my role to stand in the pulpit exhorting people in the congregation and the television and radio audience to give their hearts to Jesus. The gravity of my new responsibility gripped my heart. I realized that even though I knew the vocabulary and all the proper terminology, I had not been taking my responsibility as a believer seriously enough. And during the first altar calls I gave as pastor, I found that the words did not flow as easily as I had imagined they would.

It's one thing to sit in a congregation and listen to a message being recited and quite another to find oneself in the role of shepherd, especially when the flock you are now overseeing is the same one your father so capably ministered to for more than half a century. As I began to better grasp the seriousness of altar calls and my newfound duties, the gospel began to take on an even deeper and more powerful meaning to me. I'm sure that virtually every pastor understands this: once you step into this role, you experience more fully the burdens and the cares of your congregation. You begin to empathize in startling new ways with the people under your leadership.

For me the feeling was compounded because I had known hundreds of our church families and members for years in my various roles as pastor's son, youth organizer, college student, executive pastor, and friend. Suddenly, though, I was stepping into bigger shoes, and my perspectives on these people began to change. My heart started changing in dramatic ways too. I had a fresh desire to be the pastor these people needed—people now looking to me for leadership. I saw others' needs in ways I never imagined I could.

I felt a new and insatiable passion for the souls of all the people in our church, and I wanted to see God meet their needs. I sought to become the man God wanted me to be so that I might become the pastor my church needed. My fervent desire was to share the gospel of Jesus Christ with everyone I met. I wanted to tell them about God's saving grace in clear, simple, and compelling terms. I made it my mission to ensure that all I said and did drew people to Jesus Christ.

Yet in this, most of all, it is "Not I, but Christ."

No amount of effort or sincerity on my part can bring people to salvation in Christ. I can't coax or convince them through my own efforts to trust in Jesus. Salvation has never been dependent on human efforts, but rather on God's free gift.

I have learned that I must do my part so that God can do his. And my part is to introduce people to the truth—then stand back and let the power of that truth open their eyes and hearts and change people from the inside out.

Knowing the Truth

JESUS SAID, "You will know the truth, and the truth will set you free" (John 8:32). How can we know this truth that will set us spiritually free?

God's Word: The Sourcebook of Truth

LOOK AT what immediately prefaced Jesus' statement about knowing the truth: "You are truly my disciples if you remain faithful to my teachings. And you will know the truth, and the truth will set you free" (John 8:31–32). So truth can be discovered through "the teachings of Jesus or, more broadly, through the teachings of God's Word, the Bible. This concept is clear throughout the Bible.

Note these verses from the book of Psalms that reinforce that God's Word is how the God of all truth communicates that truth to mortals like us:

- "Lead me by your truth and teach me, for you are the God who saves me. All day long I put my hope in you." (Psalm 25:5)
- "Open my eyes to see the wonderful truths in your instructions." (Psalm 119:18)
- "The very essence of your words is truth; all your just regulations will stand forever." (Psalm 119:160)
- "Make them holy by your truth; teach them your word, which is truth." (John 17:17)

God is indeed the source of truth, and it is his truth that serves as the foundation and support for the human soul, even in the most desperate times of need.

The Living Word of God: Jesus Christ, Truth Incarnate

JUST AS the written Word of God is the sourcebook of God's truth, so Jesus is the living Word (identified in John 1), the ultimate living example of God's truth. More than twenty times in the book of John alone, Jesus is quoted prefacing his teaching with the phrase, "I tell you the truth . . ." Dozens more times in John we find Jesus speaking of the truth or things that are true. In John 14:6 Jesus went a step further. He revealed that his relationship with the truth went beyond just *speaking* the truth to actually *being* the truth: "I am the way, the truth, and the life. No one can come to the Father except through me."

The Holy Spirit: Our Guide to Truth

THE HOLY Spirit is who reveals truth and makes it come alive to us when we read it in God's Word and in the teachings and life of Jesus. Jesus promised his followers: "When the Spirit of truth comes, he will guide you into all truth" (John 16:13). It is the Holy Spirit who draws people to Jesus and convinces them of the truth that they need salvation through him: "He [the Spirit] will convict the world of its sin, and of God's righteousness, and of the coming judgment" (John 16:8).

The Truth for Believers

GOD IS the source of all truth. God's Word teaches his truth. Jesus embodies God's truth. The Holy Spirit leads us into that truth. So do we as Christians still have a responsibility in this process? Yes!

Beyond wanting to share the truth with others, it's important that we embody the truth in our lives. You see, when trouble comes, what brings the greatest comfort is knowing that the truth of Christ is within us. This truth is as real as knowing an actual person. It's as dependable as a friend. The comfort of knowing Jesus Christ in our lives does not come simply from believing a concept or theory or from following a formula. This inexpressible comfort comes by intimately and personally knowing a person. That person is Jesus Christ. I think it's important to observe that the same person who said these powerful words—"You will know the truth, and the truth will set you free" (John 8:32)—is the same person who said, "I am the way, the truth, and the life. No one can come to the Father except through me" (John 14:6). Having full confidence that our salvation comes from having an intimate relationship with Jesus Christ is what will transform our hearts, permeate our minds, and uplift our souls.

Along with understanding the source of our salvation, I believe we need to also acknowledge the truth about ourselves. That truth is this: we are nothing without Christ in us. Literally nothing. Until we acknowledge this truth and our desperate need for Jesus Christ to be in control of every aspect of our lives, I really don't believe our hearts can be fully transformed. We must remember, as Paul tells us in 1 Corinthians 6, that we were once sinners, and no sinner or anyone unrighteous could ever inherit the kingdom of God. Such were we until we were "sanctified" and "justified in the name of the Lord Jesus and by the Spirit of our God" (verse 11 NKJV).

The following seven-point "Summary of Salvation" is from my father's notes. I've heard him recite this inventory of spiritual truths on many occasions. The words have much more impact on me now that I view them through the lens of a senior pastor and not through the immature eyes of a young man who never fully appreciated their real meaning. They have come to truly inspire me because they contain wonderful truths that my father used as guiding lights during his amazing life.

A Summary of Salvation

1. Understand that you are nothing but a sinner.

"EVERYONE HAS sinned; we all fall short of God's glorious standard" (Romans 3:23).

This means we are all spiritually "lost." If we were to stop right here, the entire world would be hopelessly lost, because the Bible has just told us that no one is perfect and holy like God. Because we have fallen short (don't measure up) to God's holiness, we all have sin in our hearts, and we all are going to be punished for that sin. There's nothing we can humanly do about it.

The reason I pause here is that a gift is really not appreciated unless it really sinks in how much we need it. If I stop right now, there is no hope, no peace, no comfort, no joy, and no salvation. And I have found that in order to be saved, we have to first come to the realization that we are lost.

Fortunately for us all, the Bible doesn't stop here. There is hope.

2. Believe that Jesus' sacrifice on the cross was sufficient to pay for your sins.

"THE WAGES of sin is death, but the free gift of God is eternal life through Christ Jesus our Lord" (Romans 6:23).

God is holy, and he must therefore punish sin. God can never allow sin to slip past him unnoticed. He must punish it, and he will. But again, there is hope. Jesus has taken the punishment for us—he paid for our sin with his own death.

3. Recognize that we cannot earn our salvation. It is a free gift from God.

"GOD SAVED you by his grace when you believed. And you can't take credit for this; it is a gift from God. Salvation is not a reward for the good things we have done, so none of us can boast about it" (Ephesians 2:8–9).

"He saved us, not because of the righteous things we had done, but because of his mercy. He washed away our sins, giving us a new birth and new life through the Holy Spirit" (Titus 3:5).

"God showed his great love for us by sending Christ to die for us while we were still sinners" (Romans 5:8). God literally came to this earth in the flesh of humanity to provide a way in which we can have peace with him.

4. Know that Jesus is indeed God.

" 'I s IT easier to say, "Your sins are forgiven," or "Stand up and walk"? So I will prove to you that the Son of Man has the authority on earth to forgive sins.' Then Jesus turned to the paralyzed man and said, 'Stand up, pick up your mat, and go home!' " (Matthew 9:5–6).

5. Believe that Jesus physically rose from the dead, proving that he can conquer both physical and spiritual death.

"I PASSED on to you what was most important and what had also been passed on to me. Christ died for our sins, just as the Scriptures said. He was buried, and he was raised from the dead on the third day, just as the Scriptures said. He was seen by Peter and then by the Twelve. After that, he was seen by more than 500 of his followers at one time, most of whom are still alive, though some have died. Then he was seen by James and later by all the apostles. Last of all, as though I [Paul] had been born at the wrong time, I also saw him" (1 Corinthians 15:3–8).

6. Place your trust in his promise to save you.

"I F Y O U confess with your mouth that Jesus is Lord and believe in your heart that God raised him from the dead, you will be saved. For it is by believing in your heart that you are made right with God, and it is by confessing with your mouth that you are saved. As the Scriptures tell us, 'Anyone who trusts in him will never be disgraced.'

Jew and Gentile are the same in this respect. They have the same Lord, who gives generously to all who call on him. For 'Everyone who calls on the name of the LORD will be saved' " (Romans 10:9–13).

7. *Know that God will never let you go.*

"I AM convinced that nothing can ever separate us from God's love. Neither death nor life, neither angels nor demons, neither our fears for today nor our worries about tomorrow—not even the powers of hell can separate us from God's love. No power in the sky above or in the earth below—indeed, nothing in all creation will ever be able to separate us from the love of God that is revealed in Christ Jesus our Lord" (Romans 8:38–39).

The Bible is filled with God's promises of security. Here's another: "My sheep listen to my voice; I know them, and they follow me. I give them eternal life, and they will never perish. No one can snatch them away from me, for my Father has given them to me, and he is more powerful than anyone else. No one can snatch them from the Father's hand. The Father and I are one" (John 10:27–30).

Sharing the Gift

THE BIBLE paints a beautiful picture of God's love for people and his invitation for anyone—everyone—to come into his house. In Luke 14:16–23 we read Jesus' parable of the great feast:

> A man prepared a great feast and sent out many
> invitations. When the banquet was ready, he sent his
> servant to tell the guests, "Come, the banquet is ready."
> But they all began making excuses. One said, "I have just

bought a field and must inspect it. Please excuse me."
Another said, "I have just bought five pairs of oxen, and I
want to try them out. Please excuse me." Another said, "I
now have a wife, so I can't come."

The servant returned and told his master what they
had said. His master was furious and said, "Go quickly
into the streets and alleys of the town and invite the poor,
the crippled, the blind, and the lame." After the servant
had done this, he reported, "There is still room for more."
So his master said, "Go out into the country lanes and
behind the hedges and urge anyone you find to come, so
that the house will be full."

The key phrase here is "so that the house will be full." That's the
reason we have church. We don't want to just have a great big club
for people who enjoy getting together a few times a week so they can
feel good about themselves. The church's purpose is not simply to
have great music and great fellowship. That's not what God wants in
his church. He wants us to be passionate about going out and bring-
ing others in so that they can hear about the truth of Jesus Christ
and how he wants to live in their hearts and transform their lives.

Our responsibility as Christians is not just to grow in our faith or
to increase our knowledge of the Bible or to have a powerful prayer
life or to fellowship with other believers or to live a worshipful life.
Those are all wonderful things in terms of our relationship with
God. But we have a further responsibility to tell others what we've
experienced with God at the helm of our lives.

The more we tell others about Jesus, the more others will want to
experience what Christ can do in their lives. Let me share with you
another truth about witnessing for the Lord. When you talk to others

about Jesus, you can literally feel his presence in your heart as he guides your words and directs your path. It's an amazing experience! When we reaffirm our passion to proclaim the name of Jesus in all that we say and do, we will feel his power and presence in our lives. I believe that everyone who claims Jesus Christ as Savior should be actively representing him in all that they do.

The fact is this: many in our world do not know the peace of Christ in their lives. So many lives are in shambles. So many people live each day with no direction, no peace, no joy, and no hope of a brighter tomorrow. Marriages are falling apart. Families are crumbling. People are lonely and empty because they don't know the joy that Christ can bring into their lives. They find no answers in the culture or through education. They get no solutions from politicians or pundits. They find no peace in the stars. They find no fulfillment in empty relationships. But there is hope. Jesus is the only answer, and we are his representatives. We must tell people about the Son of the living God.

Several years ago I traveled to Florida with my dad, who was scheduled to appear in a debate with a well-known person in the entertainment industry. This was a person who had often criticized Dad and, far more troubling, had blasphemed God in ways I will not repeat. At the conclusion of the debate, Dad announced that we were going to have lunch with this individual.

As I sat at the table and heard these two men talk as friends would over lunch, I was stunned. They discussed the same kinds of things I would have discussed with people who were dear friends. They talked about politics, food, sports, and even the quality of American cars (my dad was championing the GMC Suburban). I was amazed at how two people from opposite ends of the religious and political spectrum could still have a normal conversation and, in some way, a friendship.

Later that day I asked Dad how he could befriend someone who was so adamantly opposed to everything he stood for, what he had preached for so many years, and about which he was so passionate. Dad looked at me and gave me an answer that will forever be burned on my heart. "Jonathan," he said, "one of these days that guy will come to a time in his life where he needs help. He will be searching for something that will give him meaning in life, something that will give him hope. In his position, he will probably pick up the phone and make one phone call to find that hope. I want to be that phone call so that I can share with him the hope of salvation."

That's the passion that should be in every heart—wanting, not just for ourselves but for others, the truth that can make us free. And that truth is found only in Christ.

It is this great truth of salvation that gives me comfort every day, no matter what problems I face, no matter the hardships that come my way, no matter how deep my valleys or how steep my mountains. My father believed this truth, and so do I. My prayer is that if you are read-ing this book without yet having a personal relationship with Jesus Christ, you will see your need for the Savior. I pray that you will be-lieve this truth and ask Jesus to save you right now. It's not something you can do on your own. It's not your human effort, but God's free gift. As Paul explained it, "God's free gift leads to our being made right with God, even though we are guilty of many sins" (Romans 5:16).

If you already have been saved by faith in Jesus Christ, the salva-tion message is still of utmost importance for you to understand so that you can share it with others. Time is growing short. The salva-tion of people's eternal souls must be of primary concern to us as in-dividuals and as a church. Heed Paul's warning to the Romans: "This is all the more urgent, for you know how late it is; time is running out. Wake up, for our salvation is nearer now than when we first be-lieved" (Romans 13:11).

Study the seven steps of salvation presented in this chapter. Learn them well. Grow comfortable communicating them. Practice articulating your personal testimony of what God has done for you. Then pray that God will open your eyes to the opportunities around you to share your faith with those who cross your path. They're waiting for you to help them choose life . . . to help them choose Christ. "Thousands upon thousands are waiting in the valley of decision" (Joel 3:14). How long must they wait?

WHEN YOU were in school, did you ever take a test to which you did not know the answers? Your ears began to burn with embarrassment. Your palms began to sweat. Your face turned red with the realization that either through miscommunication or lack of preparation, this was going to be a tough exam. Do you also realize that one day you will stand before the King of kings and the Lord of lords (Jesus Christ) for your final exam? He will ask you a very important question on that day, and there is only one correct answer. The question is, Did you place your faith and trust for your salvation in Christ alone? There is only one answer that will secure the favor and grace of God: Yes.

Jesus came to this earth to die on the cross for our sins, and we are to receive this gift by asking Jesus to forgive us our sins and to come into our lives and take control. When we pray a simple prayer like this: "Dear Jesus, I believe that you died on the cross for me. I believe that you paid the penalty for my sins and I believe that you rose again from the dead. I ask that you forgive me of my sins, and I give my life to you." When we pray a prayer like this, he will not only cleanse us of our sins, but he will also come into our lives. This final question will be on the final exam, but we must prepare for the final exam today. The Bible says that "today is the day of salvation" (2 Corinthians 6:2). Don't put off accepting Christ, because we are not promised tomorrow. There are many tests in life, but this is one test that you don't want to leave to chance. Call upon the Lord today to save you!

QUESTIONS TO ASK

1. What is the best Christmas present you have ever received?
2. When you received this great gift, did you want to tell others about the gift?
3. Jesus is the greatest gift ever given to the world. What will you do with the greatest gift given to the world?

UPWARD LOOK:

Dear God, thank you for the giving the greatest gift ever given to man. Help me not to keep this priceless treasure hidden from others. Help me to share Jesus with my family and my friends. Give me the wisdom and courage to share Jesus without fear. In Jesus' name, amen.

12

Not My Life, but Christ's

THE PHRASE "LIFE is hard" had been a catchphrase I'd not paid much attention to until May 15, 2007. On that day, as I have detailed in this book, everything changed for me. That phrase took on new meaning that day, as did another phrase: "Not I, but Christ." It became the one great truth that has sustained me, protected me, nourished me, and brought me to my knees as a man suddenly aware that he is literally nothing without completely placing his life and future in the nail-scarred hands of Jesus.

My objective in writing this book is to humbly encourage you to also pursue Christ no matter the cost. The truth of "Not I, but Christ" will literally transform your life if you will commit to it. I understand that the pledge to place Christ first in our lives is one that's easy to say but difficult to live. But I truly believe that we can change our culture and impact the entire world if even a handful of Christians would make this firm commitment for their lives. The disciples and the early church were accused of turning the world upside down (see Acts 17:6 NKJV). There's every reason to believe that we can do the same.

Sure, life is hard. It's full of challenges, ordeals, and hardships that derail us from pursuing our goals and test our faith. Further, Satan is determined to halt the endeavors of believers who are walking in the light of Christ. He's working overtime to cause our destruction, our pain, our sorrow, and our ultimate failure. If we are serving God, it's practically guaranteed that Satan will put us in his crosshairs. And we may eventually face life crises as intense as those of Job. It's how we respond to those challenges that will determine how much we accomplish for Christ in our lives.

The sole purpose of this book is to draw you closer to God so that you're prepared to let him guide you through the inevitable struggles of life. Fair-weather Christianity won't cut it. Only by keeping our hearts and minds fully on God can we hope to make a lasting impact on our families, our friends, our neighbors, our churches, and our culture—all for his glory.

We should prepare ourselves every day to face a challenge. First Peter 5:8 warns: "Stay alert! Watch out for your great enemy, the devil. He prowls around like a roaring lion, looking for someone to devour." Satan is very real, and he's waging a very real war against Christians. His wicked purpose is to identify our vulnerabilities and influence us at our weakest moments. In your difficulties he'll whisper that God has abandoned you. He wants to break you so that you'll never experience the hope and the glorious victory that Jesus Christ can bring into your life, even in your darkest days.

I'm a great fan of National Geographic television specials that let viewers vicariously experience thrilling journeys in places like Africa. I've enjoyed watching the gripping tales of the struggle for survival by wildlife in some of the most inhospitable places on earth. Many of these programs were made by filmmakers who spent many weeks, sometimes months, in some of the worst living conditions imaginable so that they could capture on film the spellbinding and dramatic quests for survival.

One broadcast followed the story of a lion prowling the great expanse of the African savannah. I watched, transfixed, as the great cat prowled the plains in search of its next meal. I was riveted to the screen as the lion hid in a patch of high grass that allowed it to study some potential prey: a group of gazelles that were grazing in the afternoon sun, oblivious to the danger lurking nearby.

The lion stealthily moved through the grass, knowing that the slightest sound would scare off its chosen victims. It studied the gazelles, looking for its best opportunity for success—the weakest member of the herd. Finally, after a prolonged and hushed pursuit, the lion lunged with unbelievable power and speed straight toward the gazelles. As soon as the lion shot out from the grasses, the entire herd of gazelles sprang from its position, running with incredible speed and agility. The lion instinctively knew that it probably couldn't catch the fastest, healthiest, most alert gazelles; so it focused on the one it had determined was the most vulnerable to attack. The race was on, and the gazelles were running for their lives. They knew that one stumble or one slipup would mean certain death.

The lion made a shrewd choice that day. It tracked down a slower gazelle, sank its claws into the haunches of its prey, and dragged it to the ground. While it was a shocking scene, it also amazed me that the lion instinctively knew how best to succeed: the best time to attack, the importance of staying focused on the weakest target during the chase, and how to bring a gazelle to the ground. Unfortunately for the gazelle, the lion was the victor. And it devoured its prey.

This is a striking picture of how Satan stalks and seeks to attack believers. Just as that lion quietly moved through the tall grass, carefully hidden from the view of its unsuspecting prey while waiting for the perfect moment to attack, so Satan is lurking in the shadows, waiting to pounce on us. We are no match for him without Jesus Christ to defend us. The challenges of life give Satan the perfect opportunity to pounce on us, because our hearts, in their weaknesses, are just as vulnerable as was that weak gazelle. Satan observes us during our times of spiritual testing, furtively plotting to destroy us. He wants to feast on our souls.

Satan's malevolent, relentless quest to destroy us is one of the most pressing reasons we should seek God's strength and help when we find ourselves in any trial or difficult situation. Many times we see no reason to seek God when everything's going well. We complacently tend to forget God when we're not urgently needing his help. Yet even at those times we must be alert and cautious, never letting down our guard even for a moment. We must be like soldiers preparing for battle. When the challenges of life hit us like a Bradley tank, our relationship with Christ must already be robust.

Satan is the great destroyer, but our God is the great deliverer. And while the Bible warns us that Satan persistently seeks to devour us, it also gives us a great promise. John 10:10 quotes Jesus: "The thief's purpose is to steal and kill and destroy." Satan is the thief in this verse. It accurately summarizes his plan to move covertly against us, stealing and destroying everything good in our lives. Thankfully, Jesus didn't stop there. He continued: "My purpose is to give them a rich and satisfying life."

This is the great hope that can sustain you, no matter what you are experiencing. It's not God's plan to let Satan destroy us. God loves us so much that he has provided for us an avenue of safety and salvation. He wants to give us life far greater than we would dare hope for or imagine for ourselves. Realizing that we can't make it through life under our own power is not a sign of weakness, as I initially believed it was in my own life following my father's death. Rather, this realization helps us understand our need for God's greater power, which will take us beyond ourselves into the richness and fullness of life in him.

When I think of the typical Christian who is going through life without depending on God, I picture in my mind a weary traveler. In the course of his journey, he persists in turning down the offer of aid and assistance. "No thanks," the traveler says, continuing on into the darkness and the unknown. Too many people are broken down on the figurative side of the road. To them, life seems hopeless. They wander aimlessly, without purpose or plan. Satan doesn't even need to stalk such people: they're walking directly into his path. Yet some still refuse to accept the help of a Friend, even as he continues to reach out to help them. God longs to take us into his arms at all times, and I believe especially during the times of our greatest need. Jesus expressed this unrequited longing: "How often I have wanted to gather your children together as a hen protects her chicks beneath her wings, but you wouldn't let me. And now, look, your house is abandoned and desolate" (Matthew 23:37–38).

If only we would be willing to look to the giver of life and accept the help he so willingly offers. James 4:8 says, "Come close to God, and God will come close to you. Wash your hands, you sinners; purify your hearts, for your loyalty is divided between God and the world." We must be willing to give ourselves over to God . . . to acknowledge that it's not our life, but his. To accept his help and experience his hope, we must draw near to him.

Though we need God's help if we are to survive life's rough-and-tumble journey, we have a role to play as well. We cannot simply ask him to help us while we sit back and relax. We must actively cleanse our hearts and lives of sin, those things out of harmony with the teachings in God's Word. We must dedicate ourselves to holiness. We must pursue lives that follow his will and his way. We cannot allow our slipups to drag us down. Too many people seek God's intervention only when faced with life-shattering events in which they have no alternative means of deliverance. And too many of us want God to provide solutions in our lives, but we aren't willing to follow his purpose for our lives.

We must not view God as an emergency escape hatch. His promises throughout the Bible are for both the good times and the bad times, the mountaintops as well as the valleys of life. We prepare to face the challenges of life when we seek his will, follow his commandments, and boldly live out our faith on a daily basis.

A few years ago my son received an all-terrain vehicle as a gift from my brother. It's a small four-wheeler, but it's pretty powerful. Jonathan Jr. was thrilled when he received this gift. He started riding it immediately. But in the ensuing weeks, because of family schedules and school, he wasn't able to ride it as often as he wanted. When he finally did go out to ride again, he found that the ATV wouldn't start. He tried and tried but couldn't get it to turn over. I couldn't get it to start either: the battery had lost its charge. My son asked me to charge the battery so he could ride it the next day. I didn't have the necessary equipment, but I promised that we'd find one in the coming days.

Finally we got the proper charger and connected it to the ATV. We left it plugged in overnight, hoping that the following day we would find the battery fully charged. Unfortunately, the ATV still wouldn't start. The battery was completely dead.

Several days later I got a new battery from the motorcycle shop. I went home and installed the battery just as the instructions described. I filled the tank with gasoline, and we were once again ready to ride. Jonathan Jr. rode for several hours that day and had great fun.

Within a few days it was time for our weeklong family vacation. When we returned home, Jonathan found that once again the ATV wouldn't start, and the whole frustrating, disappointing process started all over again. Now we've learned the valuable lesson: disuse leads to no use.

As Christians, we often neglect the power source in our lives. We let our spiritual batteries go uncharged. Then, when we need that spark, we get nothing. God cannot be set on a shelf, only to be pulled out when we think we really need him. We must nurture our relationship with him on a daily basis. We need to make sure we're doing what's necessary to keep that relationship powered up to its fullest so that when the day comes when we truly need his power to sustain us, our hearts are charged and ready.

First Corinthians 15:22 says, "Just as everyone dies because we all belong to Adam, everyone who belongs to Christ will be given new life." Our bodies are short-lived and prone to breaking down. We have insufficient power to make it through life on our own. But through the power of Christ, we are made alive—we have strength to get up each morning and march forward, fully experiencing the life God intended us to live because we're plugged in to the power source, God. We must never forget the one great truth: "Not I, but Christ"—not my power, but his.

What God told Paul in 2 Corinthians 12:9 is just as relevant to us today: "My grace is all you need. My power works best in weakness." Our response to this should be the same as Paul's: "So now I am glad to boast about my weaknesses, so that the power of Christ can work through me." His strength is made perfect in our weakness. When we have nothing to offer, nothing of value to give, God's strength is perfected within us. Isn't that the truth we all want to experience in life?

———

I PICKED up my dad's copy of Oswald Chambers's book *My Utmost for His Highest*—the book my dad read every day of his life, its pages tattered and torn from constant use. Inside, many passages were circled, underlined, or highlighted. Handwritten notes were scrawled along the borders of the pages. It touched my heart to look into this tome that my dad had held so dear. I felt privileged to read those notes and the highlighted portions that had meant so much to him.

In the entry for June 18, I read these words that serve as a wonderful example of what we must do to draw near to God:

> We step right out with recognition of God in some
> things, then self-consideration enters our lives and down
> we go. If you are truly recognizing your Lord, you have
> no business being concerned about how and where He
> engineers your circumstances. The things surrounding
> you *are* real, but when you look at them you are
> immediately overwhelmed, and even unable to recognize
> Jesus. Then comes His rebuke, " . . . why did you doubt?"
> ([Matthew] 14:31). Let your actual circumstances be
> what they may, but keep recognizing Jesus, maintaining
> complete reliance upon Him.
>
> If you debate for even one second when God has
> spoken, it is all over for you. Never start to say, "Well, I
> wonder if He really did speak to me?" Be reckless

immediately—totally unrestrained and willing to risk everything—by casting your all upon Him. You do not know when His voice will come to you, but whenever the realization of God comes, even in the faintest way imaginable, be determined to recklessly abandon yourself, surrendering everything to Him. It is only through abandonment of yourself and your circumstances that you will recognize Him. You will only recognize His voice more clearly through recklessness—being willing to risk your all.

The words "recklessly abandon" jumped off the page and struck right at my heart. I have since come to understand that those words are vitally important in our daily walk as we pursue Christ. Let's briefly examine the importance of those two words.

- *Reckless* means marked by a lack of thought about danger or other possible undesirable consequences.
- *Abandon* means to renounce or reject something previously done or used; to surrender control of something completely to somebody else; to give yourself over to a powerful emotion.

And so we can say that to recklessly abandon ourselves to God means:

- We follow God, never devising a Plan B. We hear his words and seek to follow his commands every day for the rest of our lives. We allow his words to be our guide and our light in life's darkest moments.
- We trust God and have no ulterior motive. We don't cut

deals with God when the chips are down. We don't put off following him until some later date when we think we'll be more ready. We don't seek him because of the hope or promise of some personal gain. Even when it hurts, even when it's not convenient, we trust him. It's not about us; it's always about him. "Not I, but Christ."

- We believe God without doubting. If God said it, we believe it fully and never doubt that we should believe it. We don't doubt his promises and never waver once we know we're on the path he has called us to follow. We consider his words to be absolutely true and absolutely real.

- We never refuse. We must be willing to serve and follow him, never resisting his leading or refusing to acknowledge his lordship over us. God will tolerate no rival master in our lives. When Moses brought the tablets containing the Ten Commandments down from his mountaintop retreat with God, the tablets clearly stated that we should have no other gods before the one true God. Nothing should challenge his place in our hearts or usurp the affection and honor that rightfully belong to him.

- We never retreat. When we seek to follow God, we must be willing to follow him for the rest of our lives. God is not looking for fair-weather friends or convenience-based companions who are nowhere to be seen in the good times but come crying for help when times get tough. He wants us to seek him with all of our hearts, recklessly abandoned to his will.

"Reckless abandon" is marked by a lack of concern for ourselves. Dad had circled those words in Chambers's classic devotion—not once, not twice, not three times, but five times over the years. Struck by the simplicity and significance of those words, Dad circled them, and wrote the date next to his markings in 1995, 1996, 2002, 2004, and 2005.

I felt as though Dad were sending me a message. I saw that he vividly understood that we as humans don't have any great wisdom or power within us that can lead us through the maze of life. He was well aware that the only way to find the wisdom we need to travel through difficult times is by giving ourselves over completely to the power of Jesus Christ. He understood that the only way to find the strength we need to battle against that destroyer Satan is through the God who is stronger than our adversary. And he understood that the only way to follow Christ is to be recklessly abandoned to him. Dad's no-holds-barred faith continues to amaze and inspire me.

JUST A few hours after the doctors had broken the news to our family that Dad had died, I was led down a long, stark hallway in the hospital. My mom, my wife, my brother, my sister, and I walked like shell-shocked zombies to a nondescript door in the midst of the heart catheterization labs of Lynchburg General Hospital. The doctor slowly opened the door and motioned us to follow him inside. After the buzz of activity of the previous hours, I was struck by the stillness in the room. The staff had left, and the life-saving equipment was neatly stored away. I felt horribly lonely.

In the middle of this room full of glistening, state-of-the-art equipment was a single bed. And there, lying on the bed, was Dad. The IVs that had been in his arms a few hours earlier were gone. The monitors that had glared and blared the harsh reality of his condition were dark and hauntingly silent. And in the middle of that somber scene lay the man that I knew had recklessly abandoned his human desires to the will of God.

I stared into the expressionless face of a man who had spent fifty-five years living out the reality of the one great truth. The words "Not I, but Christ" had not been a trendy catchphrase or a short-term solution for a rainy day; they had been his entire way of life. He had recognized the power and wisdom in those four words and had adopted them as his credo from the beginning of his ministry. And Dad had seen the miraculous results of subjugating his own desires in favor of God's. As I stared down at his lifeless body, I remembered the utterly audacious faith that he lived until his very last breath.

Paul wrote: "Dear brothers and sisters, we want you to know what will happen to the believers who have died so you will not grieve like people who have no hope. For since we believe that Jesus died and was raised to life again, we also believe that when Jesus returns, God will bring back with him the believers who have died" (1 Thessalonians 4:13–14). I was comforted in that lonely room because of the hope that comes from Christ and because I'd had a mentor who had showed daily, through his life, that this adventure of living is far more rewarding when we allow Christ to outshine us . . . a mentor who demonstrated the importance daily of allowing God to hold us close.

The *New King James Version* of that passage refers to the believers who will return with Christ as "those who sleep in Jesus." My dad had "fallen asleep" in Jesus that day. But I am fully confident that he—like those saints who have gone on before him—woke up in the presence of the Lord he loved. I know beyond a doubt that even now he is experiencing the unspeakable splendors of heaven. Today he is bowing at the feet of the Master and singing praises to him in a beautiful new voice.

I've often been comforted by imagining Dad standing before the

One for whom he lived. I envision him seeing Jesus for the first time and falling at his feet in worship and joy. And I then imagine God gently reaching down and saying, "Welcome home, Jerry."

On the day he died, Dad received the ultimate reward for living in God's strength and honoring the one great truth: "Not I, but Christ."

SOME DAY we all will stand at that same spot before almighty God. We must allow the one great truth—the one great hope—of "Not I, but Christ" to sustain us until that day. We must cast our cares upon Christ, even when all hope seems lost.

On the day Dad died, I felt as though my life and ministry had ended because my weakness was getting the best of me. I believe Satan was in full attack mode against me during those dark days. But I praise God that he reached beyond my own inability to see his one great truth and emblazoned it on my heart.

These past several months have been a process of humble but persistent growth. My faith and desire are steeped in the fact that I know that my Redeemer lives. He lives within me and calls me to do his will. That truth will sustain me until the day I see Jesus and my father waiting on the far side of the Jordan as they welcome me to my eternal home. In that moment, I'll be so glad to have lived my life not for myself but for Christ. For "I fully expect and hope that I will never be ashamed, but that I will continue to be bold for Christ, as I have been in the past. And I trust that my life will bring honor to Christ, whether I live or die. For to me, living means living for Christ, and dying is even better" (Philippians 1:20–21).

"It is no longer I who live, but Christ lives in me" (Galatians 2:20).

"Not I, but Christ."

WHAT IS your purpose in life? Theologians have debated and discussed this question for centuries. The short answer to this question is simply this: your purpose in life . . . are you ready? . . . is to bring glory to God! You were created by God to bring glory to God, by living for God. That is a simple answer to a difficult question. The real trick, though, is to understand that my life is not my life. I have been bought with a price. When Jesus died on the cross, he paid the penalty for all my sins and for the sins of the whole world. Through his death on the cross, it is now possible to live for God with reckless abandon.

Living for God with reckless abandon is not a motto or a catch-phrase; it is a passionate pursuit and a subjugation of my desires to his desires. "Not I, but Christ" simply summarizes the desires of a person whose heart and mind and will have been captured by an-other. The person who makes this declaration their direction is no longer living for self, but living for and longing for the day when he or she will hear from the Savior, "Well done, my good and faithful servant" (Matthew 25:21). My dad lived with that ambition. That is my ambition. And my hope and prayer is that it will also be your ambition.

QUESTIONS TO CONSIDER

1. The Bible says that if we draw near to God, he will draw close to us. What kinds of habits help you to draw near to God?

2. Has there been a time that you have recklessly abandoned yourself to the person and will of God? If so, when and what emotions did you feel as you submitted to him?

3. The one great truth is to allow Christ to live in and through you. How can you allow Christ to have complete control of your life?

UPWARD LOOK:

Dear God, thank you for helping me to realize that "not I, but Christ" is not just a catchphrase contained in the Bible, but it is a way of living that allows Christ to have first place in my life. Help me to not live only for myself, but give me the grace to live for you and to bring glory to your name. In Jesus' name, amen.

Acknowledgments

I WANT to thank John Howard, Denny Boultinghouse, and the rest of the team at Howard for believing in this book. Their encouragement and commitment were vital in making this a reality. I also want to thank Tom Winters and Jeff Dunn for their guidance, wisdom, and experience.

Thanks to Mark Smith, Rod Dempsey, Ben Gutierrez, and Claire Diamond for their help in writing the book. I truly appreciate all of your assistance and advice during the process.

Thanks to the Thomas Road Baptist Church staff. Our success in reaching our community for Christ is largely because of your commitment and dedication. Thanks for making my job easier.

And last but certainly not least, I want to say a special thanks to the great Thomas Road Baptist Church family. Thank you for giving me the privilege of being your pastor. I can think of no greater opportunity than to spend my ministry life serving alongside all of you.